Dumba Nengue:
Run For Your Life
Peasant Tales of Tragedy
in Mozambique

Lina Magaia

Translated by Michael Wolfers
Historical Introduction by Allen Isaacman

Africa World Press, Inc.

P.O. Box 1892
Trenton, New Jersey 08607
(609) 695-3766

Dedication

*In memory of President Samora Machel,
who loved humanity,
the Mozambican people,
peace and flowers.*

*In memory of my parents,
who taught me about freedom and justice.*

Africa World Press, Inc.
P.O. Box 1892
Trenton, N.J. 08607

First Printing 1988

Copyright © Lina Magaia

Translated by Michael Wolfers

Typeset by TypeHouse of Pennington, Inc.

Library of Congress Catalog Card Number: 87-72780

ISBN: 0-86543-073-X Cloth
       0-86543-074-8 Paper

Contents

Historical
Introduction*

Dumba Nengue *first ap-*
peared in Portuguese, written for a Mozambican
audience that was familiar—often from experience—
with the brutality that Lina Magaia makes so poignant
in this book. Within Mozambique, *Dumba Nengue*
received popular and critical acclaim and sold out
overnight. After reading it in Portuguese, and after
witnessing the devastating effects of the South African
backed terrorism, I became convinced that these
stories ought to be told to an American audience. I
was particularly incensed that the injustices inflicted

---

*I would like to thank George Roberts, Frances Christie, Iain
Christie, and Charles Pike for the critical reading they gave both to
the introduction and to the text. Professor Pike carefully edited the
translation as well. I would also like to thank Rita Snider for typing
the manuscript.

upon unarmed Mozambicans were being ignored—worse still, celebrated as the deeds of "heroic freedom fighters."

I agreed to write this introduction in the hope of creating a bridge between readers in Mozambique and in America, whom I felt would share my sense of outrage. In the process I have struggled with two contending demands: one the one hand, American readers needed some background; on the other, I did not want to intrude on the literary life of the book with a long academic exposition. Accordingly, I have relegated my footnotes to the end of the author's text, so as not to encumber it at the outset with such technical apparatus.

"*Dumba nengue*" is a southern Mozambican proverb whose point is "you have to trust your feet." Dumba Nengue is also the name now given to a vast area straddling southern Mozambique's National Highway Number One. This area formerly was quite prosperous; the peasants had clothes, shoes, radios, oxen, and plows. Today the area is infested with armed terrorists known locally as "bandidos armados" and outside southern Africa as the Mozambique National Resistance (MNR or RENAMO). Lina Magaia tells us that most of the peasants abandoned their fertile lands and profitable cashew trees after the MNR plundered their fields, burned their homes, press-ganged their sons, and raped their wives and daughters. Those who "trusted their feet" survived, but the areas to which they fled were less hospitable so that today they live in poverty.

Lina Magaia's family comes from the south of Mozambique. Driven by a sense of outrage at the atrocities committed by the MNR, she left Maputo, the Mozambican capital, and returned to the countryside to chronicle her people's suffering. Magaia's account will jolt even the most dispassionate reader. Through her, we hear the despairing voices of Mozambican

2

peasants—old and young, men and women—who have been brutally victimized.

The events recounted here are not the invention of a sick mind with a taste for the macabre. There was no intention of plumbing or choosing the most dramatic aspects. There is much, much worse. But how can one fathom it when the victims are illiterate, without access to microphones or other technology to report their day-to-day existence?

We also witness in these stories how these peasants coped with and, at times, struggled against the well-armed bandits whose contempt for human life inspired such fear.

Magaia's account also confronts the ex-colonialists in Portugal and the proponents of the far right in the United States (such as Jesse Helms, Patrick Buchanan, and The Heritage Foundation) who have spared no expense to portray the MNR as "freedom fighters" who—like the contras in Nicaragua—they claim are engaged in a "heroic" civil war. To which she responds,

And I saw my children ground, disemboweled, rent with bayonets or with their heads blown open by a burst from a machine gun. And I heard it being said that there was a civil war in Mozambique. Civil war!? . . . What is civil war? Wars, whether civil or not, are waged between armed contingents. That's not what's happening in Mozambique. There's no civil war in Mozambique. In Mozambique there is genocide perpetrated by armed men against defense-less populations. Against peasants.

Dumba Nengue is located just south of Homoine, site of a terrorist action that captured international attention. On July 22, 1987, *The New York Times* reported that the MNR "had massacred 380 people at a coastal town (Homoine) in Inhambane."[1] On the following day an American agronomist working with the Mennonite Church described how, from his hiding place in a hotel utility room, he watched the MNR "shooting every person and building in sight."[2] Other survivors reported that "the attackers shot, clubbed and bayoneted their victims." Two days later, *The New York Times* ran a story from the site of the massacre in which witnesses recounted in all its gory detail the indiscriminate killing of women and children. Appended to the account was a statement issued from Jesse Helm's Washington office in which he personally assured the American public that these "freedom fighters" would never commit such barbarous acts.[3]

The northern provinces of Tete, Nampula, and Cabo Delgado, which I visited in the summer of 1987, are more than 1,000 miles away from Homoine and Dumba Nengue. Yet the tales of tragedy there were the same. In all three provinces I heard firsthand accounts from peasants of how the MNR destroyed hospitals, burned schools, and committed atrocities. At a high school in Tete, three students tearfully described how the "bandidos armados" had killed their parents, kidnapped their brothers and sisters, and ravaged their villages.

International relief workers who had just returned from Caia, Sena, and Inhaminga, in central Mozambique, reported similar atrocities. They also disputed MNR claims that it had established health posts, schools, and flourishing farms in this region. Indeed, the relief workers reported that there were 60,000 peasants living in the area who were close to starvation.

On a national scale, the social costs of these attacks have been devastating. Consider the following: by 1985, more than 1,800 schools had been destroyed, affecting 313,000 students. Today the figure is probably more than 500,000.[4] A recent UNICEF study, *Children of the Front Line*, estimates that 25% of the health clinics in Mozambique have been destroyed and that

325,000 children have died as a result of the "war." The report attributes the sharp rise in the infant mortality rate, estimated at between 325 and 375 per 1,000 to "the war and economic destabilization."[5] A United Nations study completed in early 1987 estimated that about 4.2 million, or 31% of the total population, have been adversely affected or displaced.[6] In a very profound sense, then, Dumba Nengue symbolizes the terror and human suffering that have been inflicted on all of Mozambique. As Magaia reminds us:

> The bandits robbed, killed and intimidated. Those families who survived fled and this is how Dumba Nengue was born. . . . Dumba Nengue is clear proof that the armed bandit is a disaster which, along with natural disasters, destroys production and produces hunger, wretchedness and deprivation.

Who are these "bandidos armados" who ravage the Mozambican countryside and terrorize its people? And what of the question that the little boy of eight put to his mother—"Do the bandits have a country, Mama?"

The history of the MNR is not in dispute. Despite the claims of the far right, the MNR has no nationalist credentials. On the contrary, according to Ken Flower, the former head of Rhodesian security, the MNR was formed in 1976 by his organization working in collaboration with the apartheid regime in South Africa.[7] Several South African sources proudly claim that it was they who organized the armed bandits. Their strategy was part of a larger policy to destabilize Mozambique, which, led by the Mozambique Liberation Front (FRELIMO), had become independent only in June, 1975. Gordon Winter, whose book *Inside Boss* documents his career as a South African spy, is emphatic on this point.

5

The best example of South African involvement in the affairs of another country came in 1976, when South Africa's Army Chief Magnus Malan and his military intelligence apparatus set up a fake Black Liberation Movement in league with Rhodesian intelligence. I know all about his movement because I was its number one propagandist from the start ... It's name was the Mozambique National Resistance and when I first started glorifying its exploits in July, 1977, *it existed in name only*.[8] (Emphasis mine.)

Whatever the case, within six months of Mozambique's independence South African security, working with its Rhodesian counterparts, recruited Portuguese settlers and mercenaries, black and white secret police agents, and African former members of the elite special forces of the colonial army (GE) who had fled to South Africa and Rhodesia around the time of Mozambican independence. Three former agents of the much-hated Portuguese Secret Police (PIDE) figured prominently in the formation of the MNR. The principal figure was Orlando Cristina. A prominent PIDE official, he became the secretary general of the MNR. Evo Fernandes, who infiltrated the antifascist student movement in Lisbon during the 1950s and subsequently rose to an influential position within the PIDE hierarchy in Mozambique, became MNR spokesperson in Europe. Casimiro Monteiro, a professional assassin implicated in the 1965 murder of Portuguese opposition leader Huberto Delgado and probably involved in the murder of FRELIMO's first president, Eduardo Mondlane, took over as liaison with South African security. To this initial group were added ex-FRELIMO guerrillas who had been expelled for corruption or who had left because of unfulfilled personal ambitions. Andre Matzangaiza and Afonso Dhlakama, two former FRELIMO soldiers, received prominent positions to give the MNR visible black leadership.[9]

Thus from the outset the MNR lacked any genuine nationalist credentials. They were mercenaries—both black and white—working to perpetuate racist domination of southern Africa. To the extent that certain Mozambicans became mercenaries in the pay of the apartheid regime and its Rhodesian allies, they no longer had a country to call their own.

The MNR's lack of historical legitimacy and popular support, which is at the heart of the eight-year-old's question, did not deter the white settler government of Rhodesia from providing their terrorists with sophisticated tools of destruction. In return for its military assistance, Rhodesian security demanded MNR subservience—as is clear from captured MNR documents whose authenticity has been verified by Western intelligence officials. In the words of the current MNR leader, Afonso Dhlakama, "We worked for the English, neither I nor the deceased Andre (Matzangaiza) could plan any military operations. It was the English who determined the areas to attack and where to recruit."[10]

Beginning in 1976, the Rhodesian government provided the MNR with arms and bases along the Mozambican border and logistical support. In retaliation for Mozambique's imposition of UN-backed sanctions against Rhodesia, the latter repeatedly sent MNR bands into Mozambique to burn villages, plunder agricultural cooperatives, attack railroad lines and road traffic, disrupt commerce, and raid reeducation camps, from which they recruited additional members. They also collected valuable intelligence data on Zimbabwe African National Union (ZANU) forces in Mozambique and intimidated Zimbabwean refugees. For its part, South African security planted in *To the Point* and *The Citizen* a number of accounts of the "heroic efforts" of the MNR against the Marxist regime of Samora Machel. These were often reproduced without critical comment or careful analysis in the Western press.[11]

7

Between 1976 and 1979, Mozambique suffered more than 350 MNR and Rhodesian attacks. In the face of this escalating threat, the young nation was immediately put on a war footing, and discussions on how to reduce South Africa's historic economic domination had to be deferred.[12] Instead, the government utilized its energy and its limited resources in trying to transform its poorly armed guerrilla force into a national army that it hoped would be capable of protecting its territorial integrity. Tanks, planes, and artillery were purchased from the socialist countries as part of a national campaign of military and political mobilization.

By 1979, the tide had turned against the MNR and its Rhodesian sponsors. Zimbabwean freedom fighters, working in close collaboration with the Mozambican military, had scored a number of important victories against the white settler regime in Rhodesia. In October, FRELIMO forces overran the main MNR base in Mozambique, killing the MNR leader Andre Matzangaiza and precipitating violent power struggles among his lieutenants. The Lancaster House Agreement signed in late 1979, guaranteeing the end of minority rule in Rhodesia, forced the MNR to abandon its Rhodesian sanctuaries and bases. It was, according to a captured MNR document, "a disastrous period in which many soldiers and leaders were killed."[13]

Left without their Rhodesian patrons, however, the MNR did not crumble as FRELIMO had expected. The Mozambican government failed to anticipate that the terrorists would be given sanctuary in South Africa. It also did not foresee that Pretoria would use the defeated bandit force as its covert military arm, both to create havoc within Mozambique and to disrupt the SADCC,[14] an economic alliance of southern African nations forged in 1980 to challenge South

Africa's economic hegemony over the region. But this is exactly what happened.

With the fall of the Ian Smith regime in Rhodesia, the South African military transferred MNR headquarters and bases to the Transvaal, a northern province adjacent to Mozambique. These operations were witnessed at the time by a British military team under Lieutenant General John Acland, who was supervising the transition to independence in Zimbabwe.[15] Shortly thereafter, MNR Commander Afonso Dhlakama boasted to Portuguese journalists that South African Defense Minister Magnus Malan had made him a colonel and assured him that "your army is now part of the South African Defense Force."[16]

Pretoria's decision to take direct control of the MNR was a critical component of a broader regional policy that came to be known as "total strategy." This policy began to take shape in a 1977 Defense white paper. As Angola and Mozambique achieved independence, powerful forces within the South African military and security apparatus had argued that the prevailing "laager" or "wagon train" mentality was defeatist and inflexible. They were joined by important financial interests concerned about the growing crises facing South African capitalism. Total strategy called for an aggressive economic, political, and military offensive to insure Pretoria's hegemony over the region to defend the internal interests of the apartheid state and to isolate the African National Congress (ANC). The white paper emphasized "a solid military balance relative to neighboring states." Harking back to the notion of a "constellation of states" subordinate to Pretoria, it called for expanded economic and political relations which would link the surrounding countries to South Africa. Thus, from the outset, apartheid strategists envisioned a combination of coercive

9

techniques and selective incentives to achieve their regional objectives. The defeat of the Smith regime in 1979 and the formation of the SADCC shortly thereafter, created a new sense of urgency for the apartheid regime.[17]

It was Mozambique, however, that was to be the principal terrain of struggle and the MNR the principal instrument for implementing Pretoria's policy of regional domination and political destabilization. At a meeting between MNR leader Dhlakama and Colonel Charles Van Niekerk of South African military intelligence in 1980, the latter ordered the MNR to interdict rail traffic throughout southern Mozambique, "establish bases inside Mozambique adjacent to the South African border, open a new military front in Maputo province, and provoke incidents in Maputo and Beira."[18] Pretoria's strategy was clear—the MNR must extend its activity to the strategic central and southern provinces, thereby discouraging Zimbabwe and other land-locked countries from exporting their commodities through Mozambican ports, while terrorizing as much of the country as it could.

From the outset South African officers directed major MNR operations both from their command center in the Transvaal and from bases within Mozambique. Although it is difficult to determine the exact number of South African soldiers engaged in terrorist activities, their presence has been amply documented. Mozambican field commanders with whom I spoke indicated that they had encountered "Boers" in a number of actions in the central part of the country. When pressed for concrete examples, a young officer who had fought in Manica province indicated that his battalion had discovered several European soldiers when they overran an MNR base at Chidogo. Mozambican military officers also have photographs of South African passports and other documents captured at Chimanmane and Garagua. Sara Muchalima, a 26-year-old woman who had been kidnapped by the

MNR, recounted that a dozen South African officers along with Dhlakama were evacuated by helicopter shortly before Garagua fell in 1982. And when the Mozambican army overran the MNR command center at Gorongosa three years later, they found diaries which revealed that senior officials of the South African Military Intelligence Directorate (MID), the South African Defense Forces, and Deputy Foreign Minister Louis Nel had all illegally flown into Mozambique to advise their MNR surrogates.[19]

As the stakes increased, South African commandos no longer even bothered to maintain their facade as MNR "instructors." South African commandos, for example, destroyed the strategic bridge across the Pungue River, blocking road communications to Beira, and periodically mined the railroad lines linking that port city to Zimbabwe. On December 8, 1982, they blew up thirty-four oil storage tanks in Beira valued at more than $40 million.[20]

At the same time as South Africa intensified its military pressure, it expanded its larger political objectives. Fearing both the increasing popularity of the African National Congress (ANC) and the liberation movement's ability to attack strategic points within South Africa, Pretoria embarked upon a campaign to compel Mozambique to deny sanctuary to or support for the ANC.[21] The first indication of this policy was the 1981 attack on the homes of South African refugees, some of whom were ANC members, living on the outskirts of Maputo. More ominous was the explicit warning of South African Defense Minister General Magnus Malan in August, 1982, that his forces might find it necessary to rid Mozambique of "ANC terrorists."[22] Over the next five years, Pretoria dispatched hit squads which indiscriminately killed a number of South African refugees as well as unarmed Mozambican citizens. One raid occurred in May, 1987. In the dead of night South African security forces entered Maputo and executed a Mozambican couple whom they incorrectly believed to be South African exiles, as well as a night watchman guarding a warehouse filled with food and clothing for the refugees.[23]

South African support had breathed new life into the MNR. The apartheid regime helped to recruit the terrorists, trained them at a military base in the Transvaal, air-dropped supplies and provided logistical assistance to their surrogates inside Mozambique. Mozambican officials reported that, in addition to small arms, mortars, mines, and antiaircraft weapons, Pretoria provided its allies with communications equipment far more sophisticated than that available to Mozambican forces. This equipment enabled the MNR bands to maintain covert contact with South African submarines and planes which resupplied them at regular intervals.

The apartheid regime also helped fill the depleted ranks of the MNR. Through a combination of coercion and financial inducements Pretoria recruited hundreds of impoverished Mozambicans who were seeking employment in the South African gold mines and sugar plantations.[24] Many more Mozambicans were coerced into joining the South African backed terrorists. There is ample evidence of recruits press-ganged into service. Most were teenagers. According to Sara Muchalima, "The bandits came to my house and told my parents I had to go with them. My father refused, but they beat him up, tied my hands, and with a gun to my head, took me to their base at Garagua."[25] John Burleson, a British ecologist held prisoner by the MNR for several months, reported seeing hundreds of recruits who were kept under armed guard until they committed their first attacks, whereupon they were warned that if they fled and were captured by government troops, they would be executed as terrorists.[26] In a number of cases youngsters were forced to kill and mutilate members of their own family, making it difficult for them ever to return home.

Ripped from their own communities and drawn into this culture of violence, it is little wonder that many of the young developed such disdain for life. Listen again to the words of Lina Magaia:

During this halt, a little weakling of a bandit stepped out and asked the chief of the bandit group, "Chief, I want to kill someone. Let me choose." The bandit chief's reply was, "No. I don't want any blood today." "Chief, Chief, let me kill someone. I want to. I want to kill one of them. Let me." And he trembled as if possessed, drugged. He was crying. . . .

Rarely were the bandit chiefs so restrained. "At Madura, they came and demanded money and food. They accused some people of being informers for government forces and cut off the noses, lips and ears of a number of people. Then they told them to go and report to FRELIMO."[27] Such acts of terrorism reflected the underlying objectives of an organization bankrolled by the apartheid regime and committed to a life of banditry and marauding.

Recurring MNR atrocities, close ties to the South African regime and ex-colonialists living in Portugal, and the lack of a political program and a dynamic leadership preclude widespread rural support.[28] Successive British ambassadors to Mozambique have publicly referred to the MNR as no more than "armed bandits." And a former United States ambassador, Willard De Pree, described them as "a disparate group of gun-slingers, thugs, white Portuguese opportunists and other anti-FRELIMO types who lack any vision or program for the future."* Senior Western diplomats with whom I have subsequently spoken still hold that view. "Even where there are indications of public apathy and despair, there is no evidence that it has

---

*Quoted in *Los Angeles Times*, June 28, 1987.

been translated into support for the MNR," explained one high-ranking U.S. official who requested anonymity. A June 1987 U.S. Department of State policy paper reached a similar conclusion and warned "that it would be a serious mistake to associate U.S. policy in Southern Africa with this organization."[29] Cold calculations underlie this recommendation.

> Credible reports of RENAMO (MNR) atrocities against the civilian population have undercut its popular appeal, as have increasingly apparent divisions among its military and political leaders. RENAMO's political weakness is further illustrated by the fact that it is not supported by any country in Black Africa or by any Western Country.[30]

Little wonder then that Mozambique's President Joaquim Chissano, like his predecessor, Samora Machel (who was killed in a mysterious plane crash last year[31]) has refused to enter into negotiations with the MNR. President Chissano devoted almost a quarter of his inaugural address last November to this issue, and, as he has in the past, took a firm position against such negotiations. When I raised this issue in a 1987 interview, he responded in his usual thoughtful way, "Why negotiate with the puppet when the puppeteer's objectives are so clear."[32]

Which brings us back to the troubling question Lina Magaia poses at the outset of her book: "And I heard it being said that there was a civil war in Mozambique. Civil War... What is a civil war!?" Few who read *Dumba Nengue* will not share her sense of anger at the impunity with which South Africa, the MNR, and their friends abroad violate the meaning of language as they violate the meaning of life.

Allen Isaacman
Minneapolis, Minnesota
August, 1987

Introduction

I have four children. One of them was brought to me by fate, as a result of action by the *bandidos armados.** I gave birth to three.

When I reached home on May 23, 1985, the little ones, as always, ran towards me to greet me. I said hello to them automatically, without feeling. They stood motionless, not understanding. One of them asked me what was wrong. It was around three in the afternoon.

I didn't answer. I went into the house and threw myself on the bed in tears. My eight-year-old came to talk to me and pressed me as to why I was crying. I told him:

Bandidos armados is Portuguese for armed bandits. They are also called *matsanga.*

"Today I saw Sonyka killed by a bullet in the chest, my son."

"But isn't Sonyka there outside?" he asked, astonished.

"Yes, our Sonyka is outside. The bandits killed a child even smaller than Sonyka..."

At this point Sonyka came into the room yelling, "Mama, what did you bring us from Maputo?"

"I brought tangerines. They're in the car. Go and get them."

They all ran out but soon came back, and it was the son I had been brought by fate who said to me, "Mama, the tangerines are covered in blood. Look at the bag, Mama."

"Wash them and eat," I replied.

"Whose blood is it, Mama? The car is covered in blood," said my eight-year-old.

"Ask uncle Caetano to wash the car out."

It was only then that I realized how much blood had been spilled in the car. Blood of that pretty young girl in her red skirt. Blood of that child whom I had wrapped in my black blouse, a blouse that I could never bear to wear again. It was the blood of the children of Mozambique. Blood spilling from the wounds cut in their bodies by the knives and bayonets wielded by sons of Mozambique who have been sold out to the enemies of Mozambique. Sold to the enemies of the peace of Mozambicans. But sold in exhange for what?

What greed, what promises, what drugs could transform children of the same womb into destroyers, "brain-smashers," people who could set fire to their own brothers and sisters?

I wanted to understand. I wanted to see an armed bandit, to know and understand him. I had heard many stories. But I thought they must be exaggerated. I couldn't believe that people could do the things I had heard about. There were the massacres of Wiriamu,

Inhaminga, Nyasonia,* but I told myself that perhaps they were possible because they were done by colonialists and others who were strangers to this land. But these are the sons of Manhiça, Inhambane, Sofala... ** of Mozambique?

And I saw my children crushed, disembowelled, rent with bayonets or their heads blown open by a burst from a machine-gun.

And I heard it being said that there was civil war in Mozambique. Civil war!? What is civil war? Wars, whether civil or not, are waged between armed contingents. That's not what's happening in Mozambique. There's no civil war in Mozambique. In Mozambique there is genocide perpetrated by armed men against defenseless populations. Against peasants. It is the same as what was done by scientific means against millions in the forties under Hitler's command and what the world condemned. Yes! That's it. The excuses and the tactics differ but the results and the victims are the same. There is no civil war in Mozambique.

It was reported from Malawi on October 13, 1986 that RENAMO*** "resisters" had taken towns in the center of Mozambique. At the same time it was reported that more than forty thousand people had sought refuge in Malawian territory.**** Refuge from what? What are they afraid of? Why do they run away

---

*The first two are locations in which unarmed Mozambican peasants were massacred by special forces of the colonial army. The Rhodesian army was responsible for the latter in which hundreds of Zimbabwean refugees as well as Mozambican citizens died.
**Inhambane and Sofala are provinces and Manhiça is a locality in southern Mozambique.
***RENAMO is the Portuguese acronym for the MNR.
****Several hundred thousand Mozambicans fled to Malawi, Zambia and Zimbabwe.

17

when the "liberator" occupies the land where they were living and producing? For love of this "liberator"? In trust and hope of the benefit the occupation will bring them? Why do they run away? Isn't it a clear demonstration of rejection of those murderers?

Some people spend a great deal of money and material and human resources to spread the idea of a civil war in Mozambique. People who do this are either naive or misinformed as to what is really happening, assuming that they have any good intention. Or they are the promoters of the killings that are taking place in our country, an independent and sovereign country. In other words, they are supporting the aggression.

The events recounted here are not the invention of a sick mind with a taste for the macabre. There was no attempt to choose the most dramatic stories. And there are many, many more, some of them much worse. But how can we find out about them when the victims are illiterate, and have no access to microphones or other technology to report their day-to-day existence?

Under cover of night the killers, who are infiltrated by our enemies, are tearing the flesh of Mozambique into shreds.

Lina Magaia

The Little Girl Who Never Learned to Dream

*I*t *happened at night, as it* always does. Like owls or hyenas, the bandits swooped down on a village in the area of Taninga. They stole, kidnapped and then forced their victims to carry their food, radios, batteries, the sweat of their labor in the fields or in the mines of Jo'burg* where many of those possessions had come from.

Among the kidnapped were pregnant women and little children. Among the little ones was a small girl of nearly eight.

As usual, the bandits forced the people to keep on moving, although they were more heavily laden than beasts of burden. There was no relief; someone who could not endure the weight fell and remained forever

---

*Jo'burg refers to Johannesburg where the large gold mines which employ thousands of Mozambican miners is located.

where he or she had fallen, disembowelled or beheaded with a bayonet. Two men had already died in this way, and the others forced themselves to keep on going, to endure.

Since it was at night, only the bandits knew the way. After many trips to and from the same place, only they could make out the target. And the hours went by and dawn broke and finally there was a halt.

They put down their loads and the bandits selected who could return home and who had to carry on. Of those who had to keep going, many were boys between twelve and fifteen. Their fate was the school of murder— they would be turned into armed bandits after training and a poisoning of their conscience. Others were girls between ten and fourteen, who would become women after being raped by the bandits. Others were women who were being stolen from their husbands and children.

To demonstrate the fate of the girls to those who were going back, the bandit chief of the group picked out one, the small girl who was less than eight. In front of everyone, he tried to rape her. The child's vagina was small and he could not penetrate. On a whim, he took a whetted pocketknife and opened her with a violent stroke. He took her in blood. The child died.

The June Massacre in Manhiça Cemetery

It was close to Manhiça cemetery. Peasants were relaxing after a long day in the fields. They were awakened by violent beating at a number of doors. Those who had something to eat were robbed and then taken out of doors. Many of them were naked, either because they had no night wear or out of habit they always slept naked. There were thirteen of them.

Four were mothers with babies at their breasts. They were taken near the cemetery, to a great dip in the land left by old diggings from construction of the railway linking Maputo to Zimbabwe. They were pushed forward by bayonets, and the muzzles of guns, and at the point of cold steel, and driven into the pit.

People near and far heard shots. Thirteen people, including the four babies suckled by the mothers, were massacred, slaughtered like cattle in a slaughter-house on that night in June 1986.

Revenge, They Said

At Ribangwe bandits came into a residential area where workers from Maragra, the Marracuene Agricultural Sugar Company, resided. It was just after they had finished buying provisions. The bandits broke open doors, took people by force from their homes, and obliged them to hand over the food they had just bought.

Honwana, a worker from Maragra, was startled by the noise. He listened and understood what was happening. As a militiaman, he had a gun. He also had a bag of maize meal. He picked up the bag and the weapon and left the house. It was dark. He lay in wait.

His eyes grew accustomed to the dim light of the stars, and he could make out the group clustered around a door a few houses down from his.

He took careful aim. His first shot found its mark in the closest armed man. His second shot was in response to a bazookaman who had fired in his direction without hitting him. The bazookaman fell too.

The chief of the bandits yelled out a command: "Grenade!"

A grenade exploded, but so did Honwana's third shot, which hit its target. A third bandit fell wounded.

The bandits decided to retreat and dragged the bodies off with them.

Honwana was hurt in the shoulder by a fragment of the grenade.

Another group of bandits was already retreating with people torn from sleep carrying the spoils—men, women and children, as well as a young couple with their two-year-old child on his mother's back.

They passed cattle pens. The bandits buried their dead there, and carried off the wounded man who, according to those who escaped, died later.

They were going through an area from which the population had fled, where there were lots of wells, fruit trees and empty houses. They stopped. They said they would revenge their dead. They picked out six people to stand apart from the others, among them the young couple and their two-year-old child.

The people were ordered to climb into a deep cement well. When they hesitated, one of the bandits stepped forward and forced his victims one by one into the well.

Two more people were forced to lie down on a tree trunk and were beheaded.

Madalena Returned from Captivity

*M*adalena has returned, a child of fourteen suffering from rickets because of malnutrition. Fourteen years ago her father had been arrested far away in Cabo Delgado,* on the plateau, by puppets of the Portuguese political police, PIDE,** and sent to Machava.*** From the tough Kadjamangwana prison in Machava he was sent as an unpaid laborer to Maragra, the sugar factory, where he courted a woman. From this love affair came Madalena.

Madalena was kidnapped by armed bandits near Maluna, where she was visiting relatives. For weeks

---

*Cabo Delgado is a province in northern Mozambique.
**PIDE was the acronym for the much-hated Portuguese secret police. It stands for Policia International e de Defesa do Estado.
***Kadjamangwana is the name of a prison on the outskirts of Maputo where political activists were incarcerated in the colonial time.

and months, Madalena lived in a bandit base. The child was made forcibly into a woman for the bandits. Madalena trembles. Talking to her is the commander of the force that found her in the bush when they were searching for bandits.

Madalena has lice all over her head, her body and her clothing. The commander orders them to cut her hair and find her a place to bathe. Madalena trembles.

The commander takes her, with her head shorn and her face washed, to the brigade commander. Others present include the local militia chief, who has known Madalena for more than a decade.

Madalena trembles and holds her legs tightly together. She remains standing. She stares with eyes moist with tears that refuse to flow at the group of people watching her. She continues to tremble.

The brigade commander asks, "How do you feel, child?"

She looks at the ground without replying. She tries to open her mouth. Then the tears are released and they run down her lean cheeks. Madalena's throat is covered with streaks of ingrained dirt. Her hands end in nails that are overgrown and dirty, reminiscent of wretchedness and jiggers. Madalena has jiggers in her feet.

The brigade commander tries to soothe her. "So, why are you crying, child? Aren't you happy to be going home? Don't you want to talk about what happened to you?"

Among the people surrounding the brigade commander is a woman whom Madalena knows. The commander turns to her and suggests, "You talk to her. You women may understand each other."

The woman is startled. She eyes Madalena and thinks, "What does he want of the child? What could she possibly say at this moment?"

However, she asks, "Madalena, how did you escape?"

She replies, "It was when the soldiers attacked the

big base. We were in a small base. The bandit chief ran away from the big base and came to the one we were in. The other bandits were afraid of him and hid us. There was me, Toneca and Elisa . . . "

She can't go on but it is obvious she wants to say more. The woman smiles at her and says, "Do you know where Toneca and Elisa are?"

"No, I don't," she replies. "They told us to run into the bush when their chief arrived. We were running together at the beginning, but when we heard shots behind us I hid. We had agreed to escape to our homes . . . I don't know what happened to my friends afterwards."

"But why were they afraid of their chief?" the woman asks.

"Because they were our husbands and they said they were afraid that the chief would want to keep us for himself."

"So you had a husband? What was his name?"

Madalena begins to shake even more. She purses her lips and remains in shameful silence. She is petrified with fear.

After a while she speaks. "There were lots. One of them was named Armando. He made me call him uncle."

The brigade commander issues an order to the woman, "Take the child home. Make sure she sees a doctor. She must be carrying all kinds of disease."

The woman has one more question for Madalena: "Were there many people at the base, apart from the bandits?"

"Yes. Men, women and children. I don't know how many. The bandits drank a loot of hooch every day, and when they were drunk, they would pick out someone to kill—with a knife, or a bayonet, or hatchet or even with a pestle."

More tears flowed down Madalena's lean cheecks. "And they made us watch. I know some of the people they killed. We were kidnapped at the same time."

The brigade commander repeats his order: "Take the child home. Don't forget to ask the doctor to examine her."

Madalena's home is in the Maragra first neighborhood, an area inhabited mostly by the Maconde community. These people from the plateau far away in the Cabo Delgado more than fourteen years earlier had responded to the call to defend their country and to free it from colonial rule.* They were arrested on the plateau in Cabo Delgado, brought to Machava prison and then sold to Maragra. Today they live freely with their families.

They reach Madalena's house. The local militia commander knocks at the door of the community secretary. He passes on the news.

Though there is no telephone or radio, almost everyone hears the news at the same time. They surge out of their houses, some bare-chested, some wrapped in blankets, the women wearing cloths on their heads to shield themselves from the intense cold cast by the dew. In the midst of them is Madalena's maternal grandmother. She is old, ages old, with wrinkles on her face, wrinkles on her arms, folds on her throat, emaciated legs seemingly unable to bear the weight even of her own thin body. On her head she wears a scarf that scarcely hides the cotton that her hair has become with the passage of time. She is crying. "Nwananga mina! Nwananga mina u buyile! Yo nwananga..." ("My child! My child, you've come back! Oh, my child...")

And she falls onto the dew-soaked ground.

Madalena is sobbing.

Out of a hut comes a woman with one eye blinded by a cataract, and she whispers, "Bernardo, Bernardo

---

*The Maconde live in the northern Mozambican province of Cabo Delgado. They played a major role in the armed struggle for national independence.

my beloved? When will you come back?" (Bernardo is in Maputo.) "How shall I find you to tell you that your daughter has returned?" She embraces Madalena and weeps. Many of the women are also weeping. All of a sudden someone begins a song. A song of the people.

The woman with the blind eye whispers again, this time to Madalena, "My child, you've come back..."

Someone starts to dance. Then everyone dances—except for Madalena's mother and grandmother. Madalena remains in the center of the circle made by the dancers, but she doesn't dance. She sobs...

The militia commander and the woman who have escorted Madalena are hugged and kissed by many of those present. Someone tells Madalena, "Don't cry any more. They will never find you again."

How Julieta's Brother was "Baptized"

Julieta was pregnant, her eighth pregnancy, since she had already had seven children. Her husband was a track layer for the Mozambique Railways, but his earnings were insufficient to support his family so Julieta worked in exchange for food (sugar, flour, salt). She cleared a five hundred square metre plot, turned over the soil, as well as doing other tasks on the farmland of people who were better off.

One of her younger brothers had come for a visit. He had arrived from far off where there was talk of the armed bandits' crimes against the local people. In the Kajuau area, near Vicente Bastos station on the railway linking Mozambique and Zimbabwe, in Manhiça district, there was also talk about the bandits. But until that day in October 1984, the bandits had never come into the area.

It happened in Kamexekana. Julieta's children were

spread out asleep in the two huts built by their father.

To the north of Vicente Bastos station, the armed tramps had for some time been sabotaging the line and preventing the trains from running. Julieta's husband and his fellow workers patiently repaired the track. The trains ran. The bandits returned. They rebuilt the track once more. A cycle of destruction and construction continued.

On that night in October 1984, the bandits came to Julieta's house. They knocked brutally on the door. Julieta's husband, wearing only his trousers, opened the door. Julieta work up and followed her husband. They were forced out of the house. Julieta's brother and her seven children were also forced to wake up and to leave their sleeping mats to go outside. There was a moon, so it was a bright night.

There were nine bandits and they were all equipped with guns, bayonets and knives. They searched the main house and found some boots. They took them outside, asking whose they were. Julieta's husband replied that they were his. They told him that since he had boots he must be a militiaman, which he denied. "So why do you have boots?" they wanted to know. "Because I work on the railway and they gave us boots there," he replied.

"So you're one of those who repair the line when we cut it?" yelled one of the bandits.

Julieta began to be afraid. She was already big-bellied from pregnancy. She sat on the ground, crying. Her children clustered around her. The brother said nothing, watching anxiously and perhaps remembering some of the things he had heard about the bandits in his own area.

The bandit who seemed to be the chief looked around and saw the mortar that Julieta used to grind maize and groundnuts.

"You're going to pay today," said the bandit, grabbing the man by one arm.

The chief bandit then instructed Julieta's brother to put the mortar by the railwayman. "Lie down here," he ordered.

Her husband lay down on the curve of the mortar. The bandit chief then ordered Julieta's brother to get an axe.

"Cut here," he ordered, pointing to Julieta's husband's throat.

Julieta's brother stared, but was incapable of making the stroke.

"I'm telling you to cut here," the bandit repeated. Julieta's brother could not make the cut. The bandit, calling another bandit, told him to bring the people who had been kidnapped in the area and were waiting under guard nearby. Julieta's husband remained stretched out with his head on the curve of the mortar.

When the people arrived at gunpoint, the bandit chief insisted again that Julieta's brother cut his brother-in-law's throat. The latter was silently weeping. And Julieta's brother could not cut his brother-in-law's throat.

The bandit chief muttered a command to one of his subordinates, who grabbed the axe from Julieta's brother's hands. Without blinking an eye, the bandit cut the throat of Julieta's husband. His cries of pain went to the depths of the hearts of Julieta and her children, who shielded their eyes with their hands. When the bandit chief noticed this he screamed at them to take their hands from their faces if they did not want to die. The people nearby lowered their eyes, and a silence heavier than death hung in the air.

Julieta's husband was writhing. The bandit chief took out a knife and pointed it at Julieta's brother. He ordered that the brother be given the axe and use it to put an end to his brother-in-law's torment.

Julieta's husband was gripped by the legs by two bandits and his head was held in the curve carved on the wooden mortar. Her brother raised the axe and delivered the fatal blow. Her husband's neck was severed on the two sides of the mortar, and he died.

Julieta's seven children clung tightly to their mother, unable even to shed their tears of terror and horror.

The bandit chief said to Julieta's brother, "Now you're one of us. You've been baptized. You can come with us."

He and all the kidnapped people when off at gunpoint into the bush.

The Bandits Wanted to Enter Calanga

*C*alanga *lies on the other* side of the Incomati river. It is a locality in Manhiça district. It has a church, a health center, a prosperous population with tractors, vehicles and other resources brought from the mines of Jo'burg by men who went there searching for new horizons. Calanga has primary schools and many children.

The soil in Calanga is very fertile because of the humidity. Even when there is no rain, it is possible for those who want to work to grow enough food. And, since the population is hard-working, Calanga has maize, sweet potatoes, groundnuts, beans, cassava and other good things.

The robbers and murderers of the peasants and defenceless population had the idea of trying to rob the prosperous people of Calanga.

Through the uninhabited bush and the empty cattle pens they went, crossing the road at its most isolated spot. Silently they skirted the Maragra workers' camp well to the north, avoiding the houses where in an earlier incursion, Honwana had killed three at a stroke, and passed through the new cane fields on the other side of the Incomati.

They reached the health center, where they kidnapped unprotected nurses and stole medicines. They forced the population to carry the spoils.

They broke open the school doors. They plundered the exercise books and textbooks carefully guarded by the teachers so the pupils would not damage them.

The bandit group, confident and armed to the teeth, felt brave and victorious.

But the militiamen on this side were watchful, organized and determined not to be robbed. They were prepared to fight the murderers who just the other day had infiltrated the local state farm to burn a pump, and tear out seedlings and fresh transplants. The militiamen, who were workers on the farm, spotted the bandits moving on. They wanted to see what they were up to. They followed them to the river's edge and saw them cross. They thought the best way to beat them would be to catch them on the way back, so they waited for them by the river.

The bandit group, after pillaging and kidnapping, returned with their booty: people, food, equipment and the school exercise books. They were trying to make a fifteen-year-old take them across the river in a boat.

The boy said he did not know how to row. They beat him. The boy pretended he would take them in the boat, then jumped up and ran away. The bandits opened fire on the fleeing boy. The kidnapped people took advantage of the confusion and the darkness and ran off.

The bandit group tried to cross the river with some of their plunder and their weapons. Some were able to cross at a point higher up the river. Others remained in the river as the militiamen, seeing them return, opened fire.

There were not many militiamen. They had little ammunition and the reinforcements they requested had not arrived because the messengers had to go many kilometres on foot to reach the military command post.

It was dawn. Five bandits remained in the Incomati, on the right bank. The others managed to reach the Maragra cane field section E.

The militiamen waited for the bandits to emerge from the cane field.

As the day got brighter, one of the militiamen suggested setting the cane on fire. Everyone agreed.

The bandits were inside the cane. The flames lept high because the cane burned well.

One bandit ran out in flames. He was shot and fell forever. Others, unfortunately, managed to escape on a flank the militiamen could not cover.

They searched near the river. Five bodies were found, then another that was charred and bullet-ridden. The bodies were taken away.

Several days later, the river brought up the bodies of two other bandits with their knapsacks stuffed with stolen cigarettes, medicines, sugar and the exercise books of the children of Calanga school.

Someone said, "Let's leave these bodies in the river to feed the fish."

The bodies were still floating up and down, according to the tide.

Their Heads Were Crushed Like Peanuts

The person who approached me was the eldest of three brothers from the province of Inhambane, who left it when it was still a district under Portuguese laws. They all three came to settle in this area of Manhiça and began working for the same company in the sugar industry.

The eldest brother came up to me because he needed a ride. He wanted me to take Acacio, his youngest brother, to the hospital. Acacio was in a coma. This is how it happened.

It was nearly dawn. There was a knock at the door of the room where Acacio slept with the middle brother. They opened the door without any particular concern. Their bedroom held all their possessions as well as a suitcase full of "relief" clothing recently purchased from the company with the savings from several months' labor.

They were unprepared for what followed.

A group of armed bandits with firearms and sharpened bayonets ordered them outside. They were immediately surrounded and guarded by another group a little way off from the first whom they had not noticed at the beginning.

One of the bandits searched the house and took all the money. The suitcase of "relief" clothing was taken outside. They poured out the contents of the suitcase, bundled it up in a cloth and tossed it to the escort guards who were holding another prisoner. Acacio's brother and the other prisoner had their hands tied behind their backs. Acacio tried to resist being tied up and was stabbed with a knife and left for dead. His companions were forced to leave.

One of the bandits opened fire without taking aim. A deafening volley of shots rang out. Amid the turmoil from the shots no one heard the moans of pain and death made by Acacio's brother and another man, who, still bound, were forced to lie face down on a tree trunk and crushed as if they were peanuts. They must have suffered a great deal. After beating the two youths, the bandits went on with their vandalism, kidnapping innocent people and stealing their possessions on the way back to their base.

At five o'clock that morning I was sought out by the eldest brother to take Acacio to the district hospital. He said, "I just hope that this one can be saved. There's nothing more I can do for the other one, but at least the life of the youngest might be saved. He's lost a lot of blood but when I left the house he was still alive. If we arrive in time he may still live."

We loaded Acacio into the car and took him to the hospital. The doctor gave him first aid but his life depended on arriving in time at the Central Hospital in Maputo. A car took him.

We went back to the scene of the crime. The sun had risen. The militiamen were already on the bandits' tracks to try to rescue the kidnapped. The people had covered the bodies of Acacio's brother and his companion, but could not cover the brains splashed on the ground, splattered in blood, smashed by the pestle used as a tool for their deaths.

A Young Killer

*T*he bandidos armados have many ways to control the population whom they coerce with firearms and cold steel. But they don't always succeed. One day a kidnapped woman managed to escape. This is her story.

She lived near Madzule. Her husband worked in Maputo city. He saved money and built a cement house with a large concrete compound and an iron grille at the entrance door. Her husband's father is blind and sleeps in a traditional house. One night bandits knocked on the door and the old man just said: "Come in, come in," in time with the violent blows. The bandits broke in, searched the house, but found nothing that appealed to them.

They went next door to her house. She was alone, and lay hidden, trembling with fear. They turned the house upside down. Then she was interrogated: "Where's your husband? Where do you keep the food?"

All she could get out was, "Maputo."

There was no escape. They took her away, along with many others who were being taken from their homes. She said that they travelled a great distance, making many twists and turns. They passed a spot she recognized but which by the turns seemed somewhere else very remote.

Then they followed a route that she said led to Matrolonyana, on the way to Xinyanguanine. Finally, they stopped.

A small, weak-looking bandit stepped out and said to the chief of the bandit group, "Chief, I want to kill someone. Let me choose."

The bandit chief's reply was, "No. I don't want any blood today."

"Chief, chief, let me kill someone. I want to. I want to kill one of them, let me." And he trembled as if possessed, or drugged. He was crying.

"I've already told you that I don't want to see any blood today."

It was very dark, and there was bush all around. Some people managed to escape in this confusion. Others continued their forced march.

She had felt herself very close to death. "I can't stop thinking about the woman who gave birth to that bandit. What must she be like? What would she think if she saw her son now? What did the bandits do to him to make him end up like that?"

The Pregnant Well

*B*efore the bandit attacks began the settlement at Kamaxekana was rich. In the past, before independence, its leader was Matxene, respected and feared as headman since he was a landowner and had the confidence of the senior chief. He was also loved within his jurisdiction because he insisted that people to whom he allocated land for a house should plant cashew and other fruit trees (as he didn't want stealing from his) and because he had the Maxekane well built.

All the people of the settlement were members of a consumer cooperative, meaning they no longer had to make long treks into town for supplies. There was also a collective farm on which everyone in the area worked three days a week. This was the fruit of efforts by Celestino, a member of the cooperative management committee.

Many had built cement houses and also had made wells of cement with pullies used to draw water from the depths of the earth. Some even used the water to irrigate vegetables. Maxekane is seven kilometres from town, at most ten, depending on the route.

Old Madeu had benefited from the progress. He had built a house of blocks and cement, with four rooms, similar to the old reed and corrugated roof house he had had as a clerk in Lourenço Marques.

Madeu did not live to see what the bandits did to the village because he died a few months before the start of this story. He left behind a widow, many cashew trees, mangoes and mafurras, and the family plot where he was buried.

The armed bandits came from around Nyambi, Xinyanguanine, Bunye, Mtlolonyana and other places where they were driving out the inhabitants and turning everything into thick bush. They reached Kamaxekana and drove out its inhabitants, including Madeu's widow. She took refuge, along with most of her neighbors, next to the railway line close to the town.

She was homesick, homesick for everything she had left behind—the trees, the house, the burial plot, the cashews in the flowering season, the hope she had had of buying new *capulanas*.* She was homesick and she wanted to go back to Kamaxekana, which is an area of Dumba Nengue.

She saw her house, with its doors broken open, she saw the cashews and the mangoes in flower, the mafurras in flower. She saw tracks. She saw the well—where she lives now, getting water is an act of hero-ism—and went to look inside it.

Capulana is the Mozambican word for the one and one-half metres of cloth peasant women wrap around their waists or use to tie their children on their backs.

She says that she did not cry out because what she saw gripped her throat and struck her dumb. She says she did not believe she would get back to where she had come from.

She was running and it seemed an iron fist was holding her. She was afraid of her own footsteps even though they could not be heard on the sandy soil. In a frantic search for relief and safety, she sent the earth flying in all directions.

She said she did not believe that such cruelty was possible, that such horrors could have happened in her own well.

When she had looked into the well she had seen the heads of dead people staring at her as if pleading for help.

And the well had seemed pregnant to her.

They Slaughtered Bertana's Husband as if He Were a Goat

*B*ertana's husband was a peasant like her. In the old days he used to go to Jo'burg to work in the mines. He was young. Under thirty. On his return from Jo'burg he would hear talk of atrocities by the bandits. Fearful for his wife and children he stopped going to South Africa. In spite of the lack of rain and with great patience and hope of better days, he worked hard at cultivating the soil.

The armed bandits were killing and stealing. He heard about it, but they had not yet come into the area of Kamaxekana and the village where he lived. The community secretary asked for volunteers to be trained to defend the village. Bertana's husband came forward.

One night, he was on his way home from a visit to friends when he encountered a large group of bandits, heavily armed with rifles, knives, hatchets and bayonets. They ordered him to stop. He did. They asked him, "Where are you coming from? Who are you?"

He replied, "I've come from the house of friends in Manhiça."

"That's a lie. You're a militiaman out on patrol."

Realizing that these must be bandits, he retorted, "I'm not a militiaman. I'm an ordinary peasant and I've come from visiting the home of some friends."

"Show us where your house is."

Bertana's husband was uneasy. He did not want these men in his house because they would only bring harm. He wanted to protect his family.

"All right. Let's go."

They followed him. They trekked along, making lots of turns and never arriving anywhere. He was not going towards his house. He was walking along hoping to meet a patrol group he knew was around somewhere. But they did not encounter anyone. A bandit put a knife to his back and said, "Don't do anything smart. We're going to your house or else you're a dead man."

He couldn't lead them around any longer. He changed direction and took the path home.

When they reached his house the bandits told him to call his wife. Bertana was asleep with the children, one less than a year old. She woke up with a start, frightened by the noise outside. She opened the door and went out.

"Who else is in there?" asked one of the bandits.

"Just the children sleeping," replied Bertana.

One of the bandits checked the house, scanning it with a flashlight, but he saw nothing that interested him. He came out. He shined the light on Bertana's husband's boots.

"So you're not a militiaman and you're wearing boots? Hmm ... You're not a militiaman and you're wearing boots?"

"These boots are the ones I brought from Jo'burg where I used to work. I'm not a militiaman," stammered Bertana's husband.

"Where are the soldiers? Is that where you were trying to take us? Where are the soldiers?"

"I don't know."

At Bertana's house there was a leafy mafurra tree and nearby a thicket of bushes and trees. They tied Bertana's husband's hands behind his back. They beat him. They kicked him. He fell. They put his feet together and bound them with the strong ropes they had brought. They dragged him over the ground to one of the trees in the nearby wood and hung him head down from a branch. They tied the rope to the trunk. One of the bandit chiefs yelled, "Kill this goat!"

A finely sharpened knife slit Bertana's husband's throat, just as goats are killed hung from a tree. His blood gushed out until it became a mere trickle moistening the ground. Bertana let out a cry of grief that was ignored by the bandits. They turned to her and told her, "You'll be in real trouble if you take him down from here. We'll be back."

Off they went.

Bertana could not bear to leave her dead husband hanging in the tree. She took him down. She arranged her husband's burial in a grave close to her house. She did not run away from home because she had nowhere else to go. Nor did she wish to abandon her husband's resting place.

The bandits returned. They broke Bertana's door and dragged her outside.

"Didn't we tell you not to bury him? Where did you bury him? Show us where you buried him!" shouted the same bandit chief who had ordered her husband's death.

Bertana was stricken dumb with grief and fear. She stood rooted to the spot. They beat her. They beat her savagely in the face and broke her jaw. Her jaw broken and spitting blood, Bertana felt her resistance collapse. The baby of less than a year began to cry inside the house. She thought they would kill him if she continued to resist and so she pointed to the spot where she had buried her husband.

They beat and kicked her across to the site and ordered her: "Dig him up. Dig him up with your bare hands."

With tears pouring down her grief-stricken cheeks, without the power even to cry out in grief, Bertana scooped out her husband's grave and dug him up with her bare hands. They stood guard over her with rifles, dozens of bandits heavily armed.

Bertana's previously beautiful round features were disfigured for life.

Pieces of Human Flesh Fell in Belinda's Yard

*B*elinda is a smiling, good-natured woman who likes to dance. She has many children. Her husband was a migrant miner. He saved money and built a brick house with a living room and three bedrooms.

Belinda, a peasant woman, planted citrus trees in her yard: oranges, lemons and tangerines. She planted a mafurra tree with the tasty white mafurra fruit she's so fond of. She also planted mangoes and made a hedge of sweet-smelling plants around the yard.

Tired of going long distances to fetch water, she pressed her husband, Tomas, to put in a well, which he did with loving care. He was proud when he fitted it with a pulley and saw the water rising to supply his family. He smiled contentedly. That's how he usually shows his happiness—with a quiet smile.

A kitchen of wood and iron sheeting was built too, with a cement sink for washing clothes.

Alongside Belinda's house runs a path that leads to town. On the other side of the path is the house of Joel's parents, who were beaten to death when bandits went from door to door seeking a lost firearm. Joel's house is there too.

Joel's wife is a peasant. Joel is a laborer in a local factory, seven kilometres from his house.

Joel's wife and Belinda know each other. Both are peasants and often go to the fields together. Joel's wife sometimes draws water from Belinda's well.

It was a beautiful sunny morning in May 1985. Belinda was washing clothes when she heard a sudden loud explosion that she could not identify. Something fell close to her. She also heard a shout of pain from the same direction. There was blood on the thing that had fallen in front of her. It was a piece of someone's foot. Other parts of a human body were falling all over.

She was too terrified to move. Then she folded her arms across the full breast that had suckled more than five children. Outside her hedge a number of people were shouting and talking at the same time.

The armed bandits had placed an anti-personnel mine on one of the paths to Joel's house where earlier they had crushed the skulls of Joel's parents. Joel's wife had stepped on the mine, which quartered both her legs. Fragments fell in front of Belinda who was washing clothes in her cement sink.

Belinda renewed her appeals to her husband who was now working in the city of Maputo. She begged him to build her a grass hut on the other side of the railway beyond National Highway No. 1.

Belinda abandoned her brick house, her well, her citrus trees, her mangoes, her mafurra tree with the white mafurra fruit she could sell in Maputo city to supplement the family income. Now she lives in a tiny hut on the other side of the railway.

And she goes hungry. She abandoned her fields where she had planted pineapples and cassava. Her fields where once there was food have returned to bush. Belinda has to collect rice and flour from the rationing system in Maputo where the children live with their father.

Beside the hedge of sweet-smelling plants the fragments of Belinda's neighbor's lower limbs lie in a grave where they were buried by Belinda's aged mother-in-law.

Mandlate Died
at Prayer

*M*andlate *must have been*
less than forty years old. He loved God. He believed in
God and recruited souls for the kingdom of heaven.
He had a church built by the population where there
was much singing and where he prayed to God the
Almighty.

He had his house and church in the Manhiça
locality, near Manhiça town. When he was not shep-
herding human souls he toiled on the land and
planted fruit trees on his modest hectare.

The armed bandits arrived at his house on a moonlit night. They wanted food. Mandlate didn't have
much, but brought out what was in view and handed it
over. They saw that it was meager. They demanded
more. He replied that he didn't have it. They told him
that if they went in and found anything else he was a
dead man. The chief ordered one of his bandits to go
in.

The bandit turned the house upside down in search of food. He tore open bags, scattering bibles and hymn-books. He managed to find a small packet with less than two kilos of sugar. He took it outside. He handed it to the chief, who said to Mandlate: "So you didn't have anything else? Isn't this anything? Was it to give to the soldiers? Hmm! Was it for the soldiers? Where are the soldiers? Where have they gone?"

Trembling, Mandlate replied: "I don't know. I've never seen them."

"Again? Where are the soldiers?"

"I swear I don't know."

He was so frightened, made to look so small . . . The bandits burst out laughing. One of them asked, "Well if you don't know where the soldiers are, you know where the militiamen have gone. Where are the militiamen?"

"I swear I don't know. I don't know where the militiamen go. I am a priest of the church and I don't know where the militiamen are . . . "

"So you're a priest! How come a priest doesn't have any food? Show us where you've hidden the food."

"I don't have any more. I swear I don't. I haven't hidden anything. You've taken all I have."

"Now you're going to die. But since you're a priest, choose how you wish to die. Do you want to die seated, lying or praying? Which do you want?"

Kneeling down, Mandlate asked that they kill him with his hands folded in prayer. And so they did. From behind, as he knelt, a bandit delivered a hefty blow. He fell and they smashed open his head before they went off.

As always, people kidnapped from other houses had been forced to watch.

"So You're the One Who Teaches Politics?"

S*ome bandit bases had been* occupied by the People's Forces in Manhiça. The bandits who managed to escape scattered into the bush in search of food. As most of the population had taken refuge along the National Highway No. 1, the bandits could no longer find things to steal. The people had been obliged to abandon their fields more than a year earlier. Even the cassava they had planted had been devoured by the bandits, for bandits must eat to have the strength to kill.

Calanga is prosperous. It lies on the other side of the National Highway and the Incomati river. Bandits tried once to reach Calanga and seven of them remained in the river forever. But in Calanga there is still a chance of plundering food, and the bandits are desperately hungry. In the first week of October 1986 they made another attempt on Calanga.

They didn't take the same routes they had tried before. They went further to the north of the district. They crossed beyond Maxahomo, and from that direction set off for Calanga.

It was six thirty in the morning when they arrived in Lagoa Pate. They found the school and an eighteen-year-old teacher preparing to welcome his pupils. The bandits asked for the school director. He wasn't there.

For their own protection they had already kidnapped people they met on the way. Among the kidnapped were four girls aged thirteen to fifteen.

The young teacher, named Ferreira, was not frightened. He faced the bandits with the words: "What do you want of the director?"

The reply came, "And who are you?"

"I'm a teacher here at the school."

"So you're the one who teaches politics, saying things against us so that the population won't give us food?"

"I've already told you — I'm a teacher."

The chief of the group ordered a bandit, almost the same age as Ferreira, "Teach him to teach politics. Now!"

They made Ferreira kneel down. Then, with a hatchet the bandit cut his forehead, the crown of his head and his neck. The teacher was shielding himself with his left arm so they cut his wrist, and left him collapsing in his own blood. They took a number of people with them to cross the river. They plunged into the bush, and choosing the most remote places, led the people on a march towards Marracuene, always keeping clear of possible encounters with the armed forces. Then they decided whom they should let return and who would be taken with them. The four young girls were selected to continue the march.

According to the girls' account, it was just before reaching Marracuene district that the bandits submitted them to sexual abuse, gang-raped them and abandoned them in the bush.

Ferreira did not die. He was found and taken to the district hospital for treatment.

First Massacre on National Highway No. 1

It was an open-backed truck, full of people and food. May, 1985. There were thirteen passengers, sacks of rice, maize, tomato, beans and cabbage. The passengers came from Macia on the way to a family wedding in Maputo.

They were in good spirits, singing on their way to a wedding, as is the custom of the Mozambican people.

The truck was running along the National Highway No. 1. In Pateque, by hundreds of cashew trees that form a thick wood, a bazooka paralyzed the truck. It hit the cabin, which caught fire. The driver burnt with his truck, and only his head, trapped outside the door of the vehicle as it lay straddled on its side, was not turned to ashes.

The bandits attacked. With bayonets and knives they tore open bellies, cracked open heads and sheared breasts. Those who tried to run away were shot.

When we arrived from Manhiça, we found no bandits. They had fled. We picked up the corpses and collected the injured. Of the thirteen passengers on the lorry eight had died and five were injured.

Among the survivors was a young girl of fourteen who had a bayonet wound in the shape of a cross on her hip. She had already lost a lot of blood.

The living and the dead were loaded onto a truck that didn't have enough fuel to reach Maputo. So it first had to go by Marracuene district headquarters to fill the tank before going on to the hospital.

The day before, a bandit had been killed at the same spot. The bandits had tried to attack a miner who was returning to Gaza from the mines. One bandit had jumped onto the road and aimed his gun at the miner's car. The miner, without losing his nerve, drove over the bandit. Mastering the vehicle after various zigzags, he carried on his journey leaving the bandit sprawled on the ground.

The Pateque massacre was an act of revenge for this bandit's death.

The Lovely Newlyweds

August 1984. The bride was lovely, as lovely as any bride on her wedding day. Perhaps she had illusions of a happy home with many children, a long life that would see her become a grandmother. She was young, very young. She had long been courted in marriage. Goats and cattle had been sent to her family after the first announcement and before the solemn public ceremony.

He too was handsome. He was elegantly dressed, despite the shortages, because on one's wedding day, one must be elegant, well-dressed and the envy of other young men who are inspired with visions of their own wedding day.

The relatives were exuberant. It was Saturday, the day of the main celebration at the bride's home. There was festivity, dancing, laughter, joking between the bride's family and the bridegroom's family. There were the ribald songs that the bride's sisters and friends sang in mockery of the bridegroom, saying things like "the bridegroom's nose looks like a papaya." There were songs they had been rehearsing for weeks, on fine moonlit nights or when the pitch darkness was broken by romantic fires.

The older women (friends, acquaintances and neighbors of the bride's mother) were singing songs whose verses were meant to teach the bride how to face her new situation, songs to remind her that a woman must serve her husband, not forget her role as spouse and mother, and bear in mind that the sacrifice is forever, as marriage is a serious business. There were songs reminding the bride that she must be patient and warm-hearted with her in-laws, and treat them as if they were her real parents. They also sang songs advising the bride to have a lot of patience because where she was going there they would call her a witch, a bitch or other names to which she was not accustomed. That is the way of marriage.

On that Saturday, the women were also singing songs directed at the bridegroom to remind him of his marital rights and duties.

The bride's retinue and her bridesmaids were also beautiful. They wore their finest clothes and shoes. They were primped and coiffed in the latest styles and cast encouraging glances at the handsome young men, some of whom formed the bridegroom's retinue. The men too were in their best clothes and glanced furtively back at the girls. Flirtation between the male and female attendants is an essential part of any wedding, and the path to yet more weddings.

Everyone was beautiful on that Saturday: children, young people, women, men and the elderly—beautiful and happy because two young people were to be joined in matrimony and would thus extend the family, the community and the country.

They danced. Record players, tape recorders, drums, tins, hand-clapping all combined to produce the harmony that bodies interpreted in steady and rhythmical movement.

There were lots of gifts too: plates, sieves, mortars, pestles, pots, mats, baskets, money. The objects were given to the bride to the accompaniment of songs, laughter, joy and humor.

The bride was beautiful. She smiled now and then, but more often she bent her head with a serious look so as not to appear happy to be leaving home (one cannot reveal this even if it is the case). She held a white scarf which she passed from one hand to the other.

People were eating, drinking and dancing. The time came for the bride to say goodbye to her parents, uncles and aunts, grandparents, brothers and sisters, friends and neighbors, and the noise grew. She was weeping a little, as is proper.

About five in the afternoon a long train of specially chosen attendents began the journey on foot to the bridegroom's home. The bride's white dress would be soiled but this was what protocol demanded. So she went, the bridegroom at her side. A group of people from the bridegroom's house came to pick up the bride, beautiful, but no longer silent, tearful because she must not seem to be happy about leaving her parents' house.

And so the escort party on the bride's side and the reception party on the bridegroom's side met and danced. One could hear the songs of advice and the songs of ridicule, from both sides, on the way to the bridegroom's house a few kilometers away.

When they arrived it was very late at night. The reception committee kept them waiting at the threshold before permission was finally granted for the entry of the bridal pair and their retinue. In the meantime there was dancing, shouting, laughter, with some people keeping closer to the bride and others to the groom.

At last they were welcomed into the specially pre-pared hut, where the best chairs indicated the place reserved for the newlyweds.

Here too there was eating, drinking and dancing, but the main festivity would be on the next day, Sunday. Yet even this late at night was for merrymaking and much singing.

The bridegroom's home was made up of several independent huts for each unit of the family. The festivity would continue in the hut intended for the couple. The bride's attendants were preparing to help the bride change out of her wedding dress while the bridegroom's attendants kept him company.

Suddenly they found themselves surrounded. More than forty men armed with rifles, knives and hatchets encircled them. It was the *matsanga*, the armed bandits. The one in charge instructed twenty-one people, in three groups of seven, to go into the main hut.

Men, women and children entered the hut.

"Find the bride and groom and get them too."

The order was obeyed. Other bandits were sent off to pillage the hut and steal what there was, to add to what had already been stolen. The people who had been kidnapped loaded their own and others' posses-sions for the bandits. A sewing machine, a gift the bridegroom had bought for his bride, was taken too.

People were crammed together in the hut. Those who were outside were made to watch what was going on.

The bridal couple were still handsome when they had gone into the hut, but were sweating with fear as they were pushed on with bayonets at their backs. The door was tied shut on the outside.

An order was given: "Set fire to the hut."

The fire was lit. The thatch of the roof burned. The fire took hold. Men, women, children and the bridal couple were inside. Men, women and children on the outside stood watching, at gunpoint.

The fire gained strength. The hut was surrounded by armed men with sharpened hatchets.

The door, pushed desperately from within, sprang open. Someone tried to come out. A direct blow of the hatchet sliced at his head. He fell. On the ground he was struck in the belly with a bayonet. He died.

Inside and outside could be heard cries for help.

Another attempted to come out. He met the same fate. The bride's clothes caught fire. The clothes of everyone inside caught fire. The pole and thatch roof collapsed in flames on top of the people who remained. Someone broke open a section of the wall to escape and was caught on a bayonet. He fell and died.

Outside the horror was revealed on people's faces. Numerous eyes, in powerless bodies, looked on.

All this went on for an hour. People died. The one in charge of the mob of forty armed killers gave orders for withdrawal. A long chain of men, women, old and young, flanked by bandits with firearms, knives, hatchets and bayonets, formed a human snake weaving through the bush.

The bride and groom remained there in ashes. Their dreams died with their bodies.

After many twists and turns of the journey came the dawn. The chief of the bandits ordered a halt. He then explained, "The soldiers killed three of our men. Each one is worth seven. Do you understand?"

There had been a clash in which three bandits had been shot down by soldiers carrying out their duty defending their people and country.

Twelve Were Crushed that Night

*T*ratre, *in the locality of* Manhiça, a Tuesday, May 1985. Ten bandits entered a densely populated village about two kilometres from town, close to the main electrical line from Tete to South Africa.

The bandits broke down the door of an old man's house. He was forced outside. The bandit leader instructed a seventeen-year-old boy to take the old man to a group of kidnap victims who were being held at gunpoint near the bush that marked the boundary of the neighborhood.

The old man was forced to march in front of the armed bandit, but out of the corner of his eye, and using all his senses, he could observe the behavior of the bandit.

The old man stopped and said, "I want to pee."

They were already flanked by the thicket.

When they stopped the gap between the old man and the bandit was shortened. The old man grabbed the gun. They struggled. The gun, which was not cocked, fell. The old man punched the bandit with all his strength. His determination was too much for the bandit, who ran off abandoning both the fight and the gun.

The old man picked it up but did not know how to handle it. He ran back quickly to his house. The bandits were frightened and fled. The old man handed the gun over to the authorities.

The next day, Wednesday, a group of twelve bandits returned to the village. This time they did not go to the old man's house because they were afraid of him. They broke into the house of an elderly couple whose son, Joel, was away with his wife. They forced the couple out of the house. The chief of the bandits said: "Where's the gun?"

"We don't have guns," replied the man.

"What? You don't have a gun? Where's the gun?" the bandit insisted.

"Truthfully, we don't have any guns."

"Lie down."

He pointed to a tree trunk that served as a seat under a leafy cashew tree where the man of the house always sat to relax. They lay down. A bandit had a pestle which he used to crush their heads until they died.

The bandits left the bodies there and went to another house. They knocked on the door. The owner of the house opened it unsuspectingly. They asked him, "Where's the gun?"

"What gun?" he asked in return.

"So you don't know? Where's the gun?"

"I don't know. I don't have any gun," he replied.

"Lie down."

They pointed at the ground. Trembling, he lay down. They beat him over the head until he was dead. They left. They went to another house. They drove the owner of the house out with shouts and insults. One of the bandits asked, "Where's the gun?"

"Gun?" said the man in surprise. "What gun?"

"Don't you know? We want the gun."

"But what gun? I don't have any guns..."

They picked up the pestle and struck it forcefully against the man's head. Once he was on the ground, he was repeatedly beaten until his skull cracked. He died.

The bandits continued their macabre journey. They went on to another house, silently, treacherously. They asked the same question. As the head of the family had no gun his head was crushed as the others had been.

Another house. The same question, "Where's the gun?"

"Gun? What gun?"

"The gun they took yesterday. Where is it?"

"But..." stammered the man, realizing his plight because he had heard about the old man's action and thought it heroic. Terrified, he looked all around and saw a group of people a ways away who were surrounded by armed bandits. Some bandits were carrying more than one firearm.

The bandit inquisitor repeated, "Where's the gun? We want our gun."

Trembling the man replied:

"I don't know where the gun is. I swear I don't..."

They beat him violently over the head with the pestle. He fell and died from the force of the blows that followed.

The total number of people massacred on that Wednesday night in May was twelve.

Panic ensued. Many began an exodus at night to the town with mats, with children on their backs and with baskets holding their most precious possessions. They left their home at night to sleep on shop verandas, or in the open.

They Wear Our Uniforms

There are many examples similar to the following in various parts of the country where the bandits operate. Wasn't it the same at Nyazonia?

The shot that killed the mother killed the child too

A bandit group more than thirty strong, some wearing the same uniform as our soldiers, lay in ambush on National Highway No. 1, in the Xirindja area, at a place known as Tavira. The undergrowth was thick on both sides of the road. On one side there was a brick house surrounded by coconut palms and cashew trees already bearing fruit. Nearby was an uncompleted house of cement blocks.

A red and blue Ford truck was rolling along towards Maputo. It was packed with people who had asked the driver for a lift. Because of the shortage of transport, there were men, women, children and babies on the backs of their mothers. They were carrying the fruits of their labor to sell to the workmen, administrative staff and even the idlers in the city. There was also Daniel who had asked to be put down at Maluana on the way from town. Daniel was a soldier.

A bazooka shell fell directly onto the truck, fatally injuring the driver. The truck went out of control and struck a tree on the side of the road. Some people jumped clear. Others, caught on top of the truck by enemy fire, died on the spot.

The bandits attacked the truck. They did not steal the goods it carried; they slaughtered those who had been injured in the crash with bayonets and knives. One of the people who was murdered in this way was an attractive woman of about twenty with fashionably styled hair, and wearing a crimson skirt so lovely it could only have come from the "relief". The gaping wound in her belly made the skirt a deeper red and her innards were visible beneath her clothing. She seemed to have no pain. She did not die at once, only hours later in the Xinavane hospital—her beautiful lips painted, her face finely powdered.

Daniel was left with both legs hanging as if from a rag doll. They were broken at the thigh and his uniform filtered the blood that poured from his body.

Some people ran into the bush, many of them providing easy targets for the sharp aim of the bandits. A woman who had her baby daughter on her back was running towards the unfinished house of cement blocks, when a bandit coming towards her fired his AK and hit her in the breast. The bullet went through her and lodged in the baby's tiny heart. Death came alike to mother and daughter, mucus pouring from the nostrils of both.

There were three of us coming from Maputo. A local

person at the Maluana bend signalled desperately to our car to stop. "Better turn back," he said. "There's trouble around Tavira."

It was ten thirty in the morning, May 23, 1985.

We stared. The man was insistent, "Turn back. There were sounds of heavy shooting and bazookas."

We looked at one another and one person said, "Suppose there are injuries? We have to go on . . . "

Another asked, "How long ago was it?"

"Must have been just after nine thirty."

We set off. We reached the spot. There were soldiers there too, from the Center, who were giving first aid to the people, but had no means of taking them to town. They were scouring the bush for more injured, and found some. Other soldiers had set off in pursuit of the bandits.

It became our task to carry the injured and the dead. We were about to leave when an old man came along and, pointing at the uncompleted house of cement blocks, told us: "There are more over there."

We found the woman with her child not yet two on her back, both killed by the same shot.

We were about to set off again when a woman suddenly appeared, crawling out of the bush. She saw us. She knelt down with her hands together and begged, "Don't kill me."

She fell down, then scrambled to her knees and with her hands together again begged us not to kill her. When she saw a woman among the men she turned to me with a sigh, *"Nwananga ni pfune* . . . Help me daughter, is it them still?"

There were now three cars as three miners had turned up on their way from Maputo. I piggy-backed her to the car, and she whispered to me, "When I saw them I thought they were soldiers, but really they were the bandits."

"Why did you think they were soldiers?" I asked her.

"Because they were in uniforms like the soldiers."

We weren't worried because we thought they were soldiers

They were five militiamen who were coming from Maluana by truck. They were singing and whistling. One of them died on top of the truck, struck by a bullet that caught him by surprise. One of his fellow militiamen told the tale:

"It happened when we were arriving at Xirindja. We saw a group of armed and uniformed men coming out of the bush in single file. As they came closer to us they opened out into a line. There must have been about fifteen of them. Our friend raised his hand in greeting. That made his death easier. They opened fire and a shot hit him. We returned the fire, but we had been caught off guard because they looked like comrades. Some had black berets, others green, but we thought they were comrades because the uniform they had was the same as ours.

"When we started to shoot they ran off into the bush again.

"That's it. You sometimes hear people say that disgruntled soldiers attack the population because the armed bandit also wears a soldier's uniform. But how much of a bother is it for those who give them weapons to give them uniforms the same as ours?" he wondered.

The Life and Death of a Fighter

Struggling to protect the village

It was six in the afternoon of Sunday, May 5, 1985. The sun had just sunk below the horizon, and a gentle breeze ruffled the branches of the acacias that adorned the white house with its blue room in that silent town street. There was much joy in that blue room. Men, woman and children were dancing to the sound of a cassette player that poured out music of all kinds, but particularly African. It was chilly outside, but the dancing bodies sweated to the hot rhythm of the music. There was the sound of laughter.

The bell rang. Someone opened the door. On the porch were three men—a major, a private and a militiaman. All were in uniform. There was an air of apprehension. The militiaman had trouble walking—his right leg was hurt. There was blood on his uniform trousers. But he was calm, almost smiling, when he greeted the group of people who had stopped dancing. The cassette player was turned off. People sat down. The three uniformed men sat only after the senior officer present had given the order.

A silence continued for some time. Among the crowd was a good-humored senior officer who, noting the tense atmosphere, broke it by inviting everyone "to be less solemn." This evoked gales of laughter. Once the silence had been broken the major spoke, "There are problems, commander. We were coming from the battalion when we met this comrade Secretary on his way here. There were problems at '3 February' village."*

The happy mood vanished. Laughter was swallowed. Silence held sway again and everyone present was deeply moved. Even the babies were quiet.

"At '3 February' again?"

The village Secretary took the floor and reported, "Yes, commander. It must have been about three in the morning when the enemy moved into the third ward. People were sleeping. It was very dark. They came through the grazing area to the west of the village." He paused with an obvious gasp of pain. He shifted the position of his injured leg and stretched it out.

"But you're hurt," said a woman from the crowd in the blue room.

The Secretary looked at her in silence. She repeated her comment. Everyone took note of the Secretary's weariness and pain.

The major answered for him, "Yes. He's hurt and he's travelled many kilometers on foot. We met near Maxahomo."

"Could you treat him?" the woman asked.

---

*3 February is the day in 1969 that Eduardo Mondlane, the first president of FRELIMO, was assassinated. Many communal villages in Mozambique have this name. The village mentioned here is in Manhiça district.

"We bandaged him and gave some treatment. The bullet didn't lodge, so he lost a lot of blood."

"But what happened?" asked another senior officer.

Once more the floor was taken by the village Secretary who was also in charge of local defense. His was a prosperous village with more than five thousand inhabitants—peasants, herders, relatives of miners in Jo'burg. A large number of their cattle had already been stolen or decimated by the armed bandits. Pastures had been abandoned after the bandits had several times killed oxen and cows in calf—killing for the sake of killing what they could not take with them. They killed purposelessly and so one could say they murdered the cattle. The population tried to protect their cattle by moving them to other locations, but very often these places didn't have enough water. And so the cattle died. Most of the five thousand inhabitants no longer had good land for their crops because bandits had pillaged and burnt the most fertile spots. Five thousand people organized into a small town with houses of brick or wattle and daub, with thatched or corrugated roofs. Five thousand people with hopes for the future.

The floor was taken again by the Secretary of the village, who recounted, "When they arrived—from what we could tell from the tracks we found at dawn—they went to and fro through the third ward in small groups. They stole goats, chickens and people."

He paused, then went on, "The noise they made woke people up. To force people to stay indoors, the bandits set fire to thirteen houses." A fresh surge of pain silenced him for a few moments. Shifting his leg again, he went on, "Nonetheless people did leave their houses and managed to get to the village center. We organized ourselves and went to the third ward after one of the residents had informed the militia command. And we fought. We lost the men and women they had killed before the battle began, but when we faced them with weapons they beat a hasty retreat. They killed two of my colleagues and I was hit in the leg when our ammunition ran out. We followed them out of the village."

His impressively calm and measured voice fell silent.

The listeners in the blue room lowered their heads in deep thought. They were thinking of the unarmed victims that the bandits had killed. Each was thinking too of the thirteen houses burned with all their contents: food, shoes, clothes, money, all their owners' worldly goods. Luckily most of the people from the houses had managed to flee.

Madala Makana, committee Secretary and head of '3 February' village accepted the plate that someone had brought from the kitchen into the blue room, and slowly, very slowly, was chewing the rice with some stew. He had eaten nothing all day. Heavy silence lasted in the room while he was eating.

With the plate in his hand and a faraway look in his eyes, he continued, "If we'd had more ammunition we could have taken them. There were lots of them. When day broke and we made a search we found traces of blood on the grass into the bush. I think we got some of them."

And someone was thinking, "What? After that injury he was still off searching the bush?"

Struggling to develop the village

November 1985. A Wednesday. A group of five people arrived in a "decolonized" land rover* just before nine in the morning at '3 February' village. Two were foreigners (one Italian and one British) and three

---

*"Decolonized land rover" refers to a poem written by Albino Magaia, which depicts how, in contrast to its use during the colonial period, the land rover now serves the people of Mozambique.

were citizens. They came to find out about the village's difficulties. One of the villagers ran off in search of Madala Makana, the village Secretary. He was in the fields with the other peasants.

Madala Makana was not disturbed. He put down his hoe and made for the spot where the five people were waiting for him, surrounded by inquisitive children. One of the foreigners was speaking in his own way to one of the children.

Madala Makana approached the group. His hands were soiled and his boots muddy. He said, "Forgive my appearance. I wasn't expecting you. I was in the fields. As I didn't know if you would be with us for very long, I didn't want to waste time, so I came straight here." As he spoke, he shook the hand of each of the visitors.

One of the citizens was profusely apologetic for not having given notice of the visit, explaining that it had been made on the spur of the moment, and he introduced the members of the group.

Madala Makana understood that these people wanted to know about the production potential of the village, and would like to study what could be done to support the village.

Madala Makana explained the village's situation. He spoke about the number of inhabitants. He spoke of the field the peasants had abandoned because of armed bandit activity. He talked about the grazing needs of the livestock. He spoke of the brick factory that had shut down for lack of transport and the activity of the bandits.

He dreamed aloud about the irrigation that could be built for the plain, with flood drainage, and he dreamed of three hoes per peasant for the clearing and digging of the sandy, alluvial soil.

In his calm and measured voice he put across what the actions of the bandits meant. He recounted the more than thirteen occasions they had come into the

village to kill, rob and burn, because the village, despite everything, kept steadily growing. The bandits killed, burned and robbed, saying that anyone in a communal village was their enemy. They hoped in this way to dishearten the people and make the villagers abandon their organized way of life.

The foreigners and citizens in the land rover party took notes. The explanation by the Secretary of '3 February' village was so direct, so calm and measured, that when at the end he asked if they needed any more information, the only request was to see the areas suggested for irrigation.

"Yes, of course. It's just down here."

The "decolonized" land rover set off. It was now carrying seven passengers, including the village Secretary and the economic secretary. The vehicle roared into life and descended the plain, where the village Secretary pointed out the rich, fertile area of more than five thousand hectares as far as the border with Gaza province. He indicated the water courses where irrigation could be set up. As he said, "One must eat to live, but the others won't let us live . . . " and he added, "How many of those who are in the capital without work would have something to do if this land could be used?"

Several blank sheets of paper were filled up by eager pens. The citizens and the foreigners covered the white paper with ink as they noted the ideas.

One of the foreigners, with a strong shake of the calloused and soiled hand of Madala Makana, said on departure, "We shall meet again soon. Your dream is not impossible. It can be put into practice. It's good that you should have this dream."

"One must live with optimism," Madala Makana replied. "They don't let us live in peace. But we shall go on struggling to be free people living in peace." The village Secretary's voice rang not so much with passion as conviction.

The party of five left and returned to town, thinking, "What a man. So steady, so certain of what he wants and how . . . "

Never to meet again

The foreigners left the following day. The Italian said, "I would like to have another meeting with the Secretary of '3 February' village. I should like to be able to do something to make his dream come true. At home the necessary financing can be found. A project can be carried out." He paused and added, "See how, though he's scarcely able to read, he has formulated a plan, a project for his village's development. It's the truth, I would like to meet him again."

"And you shall meet him," answered one of the citizens. "You shall meet him. That's how the man is. He knows what he wants and how . . . "

In the still of the night after the departure of the group of five in the land rover, in the silence of the night of the peasants who have no electricity, no kerosene for lighting, no candle, who are afraid to light a fire to reveal their presence—in the darkness lit only by the billions of stars, the armed bandits tried once more to enter '3 February' village.

Their aim was to steal people, goats, chickens, maize meal, rice, beans, cassava, trousers, shirts, skirts, blouses, shoes, radios, batteries, everything that would provide food, clothing and entertainment on their course as idle tramps, murderers and thieves lurking in the bush without present or future.

But the village command heard. It was organized. Led by the Secretary who was also in charge of defense, it responded to the aggression.

The bandits did not succeed in penetrating the village. This time they did not succeed in killing unarmed people because they were promptly defended. The bandits were driven off. The weapons sang until the bullets ran out. The Secretary was wounded. Not in the right leg this time, but in the chest. He fell. His weapon fell silent without ammunition. One of the bandits who had seen him fall spotted this. He came up and buried a bayonet in the Secretary's throat, slitting it.

Madala Makana, Secretary of '3 February' village, is buried...

Nine in the morning, Friday, a very hot day in November 1985. From all corners of the district came many crowded land rovers, Toyotas and trucks to '3 February.'

The village center was empty. From various directions sobs could be heard—the sobs of men, women and children. The women had cloths on their heads, folded in a square. Men held their chins, shook their heads, shed silent tears, or sobbed deep in their throats. They were going towards the home of Madala Makana, Secretary of '3 February' village, who the night before had been murdered by armed bandits. It was the moment of his burial.

There was not enough room for the more than five thousand people who had come to accompany Madala Makana to his last resting place.

The coffin containing the body was inside the house in the room where the women and more than nine sons were paying their last respects. Madala Makana was in his prime at little more than forty.

Many of those present wanted to look for the last time on his calm, serene, beardless face, greyed in death, his throat wrapped in a white cloth, and his eyes closed by a friendly hand after death had replaced life in his body.

It was impossible for all of them to enter the house. So someone suggested taking the coffin outside.

After the coffin had been taken out, and when it was

placed on two wooden chairs and opened, then, as if a button had been pressed, thousands of throats uttered a sharp, anguished wail of despair.

A voice rang out, "Oh . . . Madala Makana, why did they kill you? How could they overcome you now? What will become of us, our village, our life without you? Father, father, why did you die?" The speaker fell to the ground. Someone went to her aid.

Another voice said, "No, they haven't beaten you. They haven't beaten you. You are above them because you died defending what we are. We do not want you dead. How can you leave this coffin? How? We don't want you dead. Who will care for your children, all of your children who need you so much? They killed you but they haven't beaten you."

A young man of about fifteen was shouting, "Papa, papa, now that you're dead, who will teach us about courage, bravery and organization? Who, who will teach us? How could they kill you? They could do it only by treachery. You could not walk properly, you were limping from the last wound and so you could not escape, as you did the other times. You fell and when you were wounded the bandits killed you. Now who will teach us about courage and bravery?"

And he wept, surrounded by the other youngsters who were sobbing with grief.

The burial was set for ten o'clock. It could not be held on time because one by one the people of the village and the visitors wanted to take a last look at that serene and calm being, whose voice was colorless, whose gaze was sombre, whose eyes were shining, intelligent, faraway, but who could flash a beautiful and sincere smile. They wanted to see those eyes again, but they were closed. They saw the white cloth, like a thick collar around his throat, and that he was dressed in his best suit.

The sun was blazing hot. The moist air carried the strong scent of the sweat of five thousand people and more who wept, sighed or were silent in the face of the grief that pierced them at the death of Madala Makana, village Secretary.

The cortege was able to leave the house only after eleven. The first steps to the cemetery were taken with the coffin passed from hand to hand by teams of ten men who elbowed and shoved for the privilege of carrying it, the last visible apparel of Madala Makana on his way to his last resting place. Space had already been dug in the soil to fit the coffin that cradled him.

Someone came along and offered his vehicle to carry Madala Makana. There were soldiers too who followed silently in the crowd.

Along the route of more than two kilometers there was much talk, lamentation and weeping. And old, old woman said, "That's how we are at the bandit's mercy. They hunted him so hard, hunted him so hard, and now they've done it. He's dead. Who will protect us? So many times they came to kill us and he protected us. And now? Must we leave the village where he taught us how to live? Must we return to a life of isolation?"

A troublesome dust, that none paid heed to, hung in the air, raised by the feet of those tramping to the cemetery.

They reached the cemetery. It was past mid-day. The sun at its zenith pricked the eyes and heads and bodies of the more than five thousand people, but they paid no heed.

A voice lamented, "How can we hide his body and the place where we bury him? Those savages may come and dig him up, steal him by night to chop into pieces or cut off his head to take to their chiefs. They were after him so much in life that they may do this in death. Isn't it so? Wasn't he wounded when they killed him? If it hadn't been for his lame leg perhaps he could have escaped despite the wound ... "

Someone else in the crowd was thinking, "Is it possible to do such a thing to a corpse?"

He had not completed the thought when he heard, "That's true. We must mount a guard over the next few days so that the bandits don't steal the body."

The village's cemetery, though it has been in use for less than a decade, has many graves. Many graves of people murdered by the armed bandits. Everything possible was done to camouflage the new grave so that at night it would be lost among the others. No flowers or specially fine plants were planted. The fear that they should steal the body of Madala Makana, village Secretary, seeped into all who'd head the remarks.

The funeral ceremony for Madala Makana was over. In small groups, residents and visitors made their way sadly back to their neighborhoods, to their homes, to their fears about the bandits, as well as to their determination to fight the enemy.

Suddenly a woman ran from the last row of houses in the vilage's first ward, shouting in terror, "The bandits are down there in the valley, by the lake. They're camped there."

From various corners of the village people came running, or crawling, loading bundles, with some heading for National Highway No. 1. There was nearly a general panic. A voice yelled, "Oh Madala Makana. If only you were here to tell us what to do."

There was a sound of weapons being cocked. It was a group of soldiers who came to Madala Makana's burial and who on hearing the news were preparing for battle. They went off to ambush the enemy.

A woman visitor to the funeral asked a woman of the village for a glass of water. The resident gave it to her and said, "They are trying to scare us into leaving the village. But we never shall. Madala Makana taught us how to live in this village of ours and if we were to abandon it we would not be showing him the love he deserves."

She was carrying on her back a child of less than two and a half who was crying, and so she cradled the baby to hush him.

Dumba Nengue
or
Wealth Abandoned

*I*t *is incidents such as these*
that have created Dumba Nengue.

The armed bandits arrived at Bunhe, the district of
Manhiça, on the way to Moamba district. They found a
woman cooking.

She had a child on her back. He was tiny, as he was
less than a year old.

They demanded that she give them food. She was
still cooking it. Since she did not yet know the murderous nature of the bandits in the area, she refused. They
told her to put her baby son in the pot on the fire if she
wanted to escape death.

She replied, "You can kill me, but I will not cook my
child."

And they killed her.

* * *

93

He was a healer. The armed bandits swear by consultations with the healers, spirit mediums and witch doctors. They cover themselves with amulets they believe make them immune to bullets.* They deck themselves with amulets which they think give them courage to kill. They take various drugs to have hallucinations that make them bloodthirsty.

He was a healer and a cattle and goat breeder. He was a reputable man. The bandits sought him out and promised him more power than he had as a healer. They demanded that he give them powers he was unable to give.

They threatened him with death. He gave them meat to placate them. They ate. They promised to come back.

He was a healer. He had many wives. When the armed bandits went, his wives begged him to flee. They were afraid of that promised return. Many people had already been killed near Mapulanguene, and the news had reached them at Ka Matrolonyana.

He tried to refuse, but his wives were insistent. They said they would look after his property, because since they were not healers, they were not the target.

In the end he agreed. He took refuge at his sister-in-law's home in the village of Kamaxekana. He went through dismal weeks of homesickness for his family and his possessions. His wives came to visit him. From them he had news of his home and how things were going. He knew that the bandits had not returned. But even so, his wives told him, he should not return home since they could appear when least expected.

---

* During the wars against Portuguese occupation at the beginning of this century, outgunned African fighters often used to take a variety of potions which they believed would turn European bullets into water. See Allen Isaacman, *The Tradition of Resistance in Mozambique* (Berkeley, 1976).

He stood it for a month. Whenever his wives came to visit they told him that the bandits hadn't come near the house again, although there had been much cattle rustling at night by persons unknown.

More weeks went by. He could stand it no longer. He took the route home. His sister-in-law, Nwaxi-punguana, widow of his older brother, and already very old (she died of old age in that same year of 1984), tried to persuade him not to go. But he went.

He slept at home one night. The following night the bandits arrived. He did not have the powers they wanted him to give them. They slit his throat.

The death of this wealthy healer was a shock to the residents of the area. Many ran away. They abandoned their cashew trees, their mangoes, their mafurras, their wells, their cattle, their cement block houses. The area was occupied by bandits.

* * *

She had just received food sent by her husband who was in the mines of Jo'burg. A whole truckload. With the food came clothes for her, for the children, parents and in-laws, and since her husband was just about to return, he sent a suitcase of clothes for himself too. Her house was beautiful. It was painted blue. It has four rooms and a corrugated roof. There was much talk of the prosperity of the Mandlate family, for she was not idle. She had fields of maize, cassava and beans, and she rented a tractor for the first ploughing.

The armed bandits, like treacherous snakes, came by night and pillaged the storehouse. They had kid-napped people as porters. But the quantities in the house were beyond the physical capacity of the carriers. She was also forced to be a porter and to witness her home set on fire with all the things that remained inside. She was made to witness the result of the fire

96

that slowly and completely consumed flour, sugar, clothing and all that was left.

When she returned from captivity weeks later she took refuge on the outskirts of the railway line, feeling fortunate that they hadn't killed her and wondering what would happen if they came back again and found her there.

And there remained her cashew trees, her mafurra trees, her mangoes and her pineapples—abandoned.

* * *

Jaime took on the management of a factory when the manager was killed in an accident. He lived in Kamaxekana. He built a brick house. He planted many pineapples and from his father, Sasseka, he inherited cashew, mafurra, lemon, tangerine, grapefruit and orange trees, and many other typical fruit trees of the area.

The armed bandits arrived at his house on a dark night. He had sugar, rice and other foodstuffs. He also had a typewriter.

When they arrived they asked where the manager's house was and he replied that he did not know the manager or where he lived. They asked if he knew Jaime and he said he didn't. "Show us what you have in your house," they told him. He showed them. They took out all the food. They asked him what equipment he had. There was a stand with a radio and record-player. They told him to play it and he said it was out of order. They spotted the typewriter and took it.

They made him and his wife go with them. They found other kidnap victims. One was his cousin, Celestino, a sick old man whom the bandits forced to carry the portable radio he had at home.

They had also kidnapped Caetano, a younger cousin of Jaime's.

They went with the bandits for many kilometers. They went through Ka Ribzweni, through Nyambi. When it was almost daybreak, they were released with this advice, "Go back by the same way you came. If you change route we will know it and when we return you will be dead men."

The daughter-in-law of one of the kidnapped was raped by more than ten bandits.

Jaime never went back to his house. Celestino managed to collect some of his furniture. Now they live in hunger beside National Highway No. 1.

* * *

It was not yet night. The bandits came armed with hatchets and knives, and some had firearms. They told the master of the house that they were hungry and wanted food. He replied that his wife had not yet come from the field and so had not yet done the cooking. They explained that they didn't want women's cooking, they wanted meat to barbecue and eat. He should kill an ox for them.

He had oxen that he used for ploughing. Others he raised for sale and to feed the family on important occasions. He was reluctant to kill an ox and did not conceal the fact.

They sat on the ground with one standing as sentinel with a cocked rifle in his hand. They repeated the order. He resisted. They offered an alternative. Instead of an ox he should slaughter a goat.

It was a death sentence. "Who did he think he was to deny them what they wanted?"

The children and his wife arrived. In their presence his throat was cut and his head severed from his body. One of the bandits then made a cross with a sharpened point on which he stuck Jaime's head.

They called the family together and said: "Now we are going to kill an ox. You, woman, will make a fire and roast the meat for us. But woe betide you if you bury the man. You will all be killed."

The ox was slaughtered. The meat was roasted. The banquet was held. The family was forced to eat too, to swallow even though their throats were gripped by anguish and fear.

The bandits demanded drink as well. When they were satisfied they left, but not before warning once again, "That one may not be buried. He must stay until he rots as a lesson in obedience."

The family fled. The oxen, the goat, the fruit trees, the huts remained abandoned.

That is how *Dumba Nengue* was born.

* * *

Dumba Nengue is a vast area that once provided the food for the people now sheltered along the National Highway No. 1. They call it *Dumba Nengue*, which means "you have to trust your feet" because in order to be able to buy new goods or replace the goods that were stolen, burned or abandoned, one has to try to return to bandit-occupied areas to recover one's harvest. In 1986, at the time of the cashew crop, only the fastest people managed to pick cashews in an area thickly covered with cashew trees. The bandits killed many to stop them from harvesting a valuable source of wealth, and only those who could run fast managed to get enough cashews for the purchase of clothes, radios, batteries and other useful things of life.

Dumba Nengue is clear proof that the armed bandit is a disaster which, along with natural disasters, destroys production and produces hunger, wretchedness and deprivation.

An Armed Bandit: An Unfinished Portrait

In October 1985 there was a campaign to scour the bush in search of armed bandits. The people's soldiers pursued, killed and captured many bandits who had been responsible for murdering the population.

I saw three of these captured bandits who were detained at a military post.

Sometimes we are afraid of something just be looking at it. I am afraid of snakes. When I see a white lizard, it gives me the creeps. Whenever I see one, my flesh cringes and I shiver to the roots of my hair. I feel as if I am being scalped.

That's what I felt when I saw those three bandits. They were black, African, Mozambicans. Born in Inhambane. The oldest could not have been more than twenty-three.

One of them stands out so clearly in my mind that images of the other two have become hazy. He was about 1.7 meters tall. He was thin, and wearing a sheepskin coat that had once been light in color. He wore faded blue jeans. Inside the coat you could see a shirt that had been red.

What made me shiver, as I do when I see a snake or a white lizard, was the bandit's eyes: bloodshot and full of hatred and cynicism. Not lifeless like the eyes of a frog, but glaring, staring aggressively wherever they looked.

His matted locks looked as if they had never been washed or cut. He had been kidnapped and taken to South Africa where he was trained in June 1985, after the Nkomati Agreement (signed with South Africa in March 1984).

No physical or moral pressure was needed to get him to describe what he had done in the three months he had been operating in the district. He estimated he had killed more than 240 people. He had been present at the massacres on the National Highway No. 1. He had killed with bayonet and knife and spoke of all this as if he were talking about dancing at a party.

The smile he gave as he spoke was an insult to the human race. I suspect he took a mad delight in talking of the blood that poured onto him from the victims and from the blades he used to draw it. I have never seen so much cynicism in one human being.

And the same revulsion and cringing I have when I see a snake made my flesh come out in goose pimples and a shiver run down my spine.

Can this be a man?

Ilda Was So Full of Hatred that No One Could Stop Her

*T*his is just a vignette.

The soldiers captured some bandits with their weapons. They took them with them through a pocket of the Manhiça area. The people saw the bandits. Dirty, unkempt, full of lice, with bloodshot eyes revealing contempt for the masses.

Ilda was among the people. She remembered her brother who had recently been killed. She stared and stared. Her hatred was rising and filling her.

No one saw where the huge rock came from which she wielded with force and brought down on the head of one of the bandits. He fell like a log. Ilda swiftly smashed in the bandit's head with the rock.

Thus had the bandits killed her brother: beating his skull to a pulp.

Mama Do Armed Bandits Have a Country?

*A*nyone listening to the BBC, the Voice of America, Radio South Africa and other powerful radio stations around the world, will certainly have heard it said on some of them that there is civil war in Mozambique. They say that the rebels called RENAMO (and many other names before this one) are opposed to the government army.

Recently, the BBC in London reported a statement by the general head of the armed bandits to the effect that he had areas of Zambezia province under his control.*

---

* During the second half of 1986 MNR Forces based in Malawi launched a major attack into Central Mozambique, attempting to cut the country in half. Within 6 months Mozambican forces aided by troops from Zimbabwe and Tanzania had recaptured most MNR controlled territory and had inflicted heavy losses on the terrorists.

I heard this on 13 October 1986.

And when I heard it, I thought of the people I had met returning from the bases of armed bandits and the tales they told of what they saw and experienced there. I thought, "I should like to meet this general who is head of the murderers of the people and ask him a few questions." The questions I should like to put to him are these:

"You lead a torrent of assassins who kill defenseless people. How do you rate this as a civil war?"

"You gave orders for the kidnapping of children of 12, 13, 14, and 15 years-of-age to be trained and transformed into killers. What objectives do you hope to achieve with that?"

"What reply would you give to this question asked by an old peasant: So these vermin infesting the bush, do they say why they do this? Do they want to rule? Whom will they rule? Whom will they rule if they kill us day after day?"

"What is your view on this statement by a peasant woman who fled from one of the areas you occupy: Their crime is so great. As well as killing bodies they kill human conscience, the essence of existence. If you saw how they live in those places! . . . Even swine, lions, tigers are more sane than a man who is no longer human. They make killers of women and even children. They spend their time drinking, seeking witch doctors, killing people. We also kill the animals we have in the poultry and the cattle pens, but we kill because we want to eat. Why do they kill? They steal our food but don't let us produce. At least if they didn't take our lives we could continue to produce and they would benefit too since they're theives. We'd produce, and they'd steal what we produced. Perhaps something would be left for us to have the strength to produce more and they would come and steal. And we would go on producing. . . . How can we do that now that we live in fear of death from one minute to the next? If they force us to abandon our fields?"

General, head of the bandits, what would you answer to this question from a young man of fifteen after his return from the bush where your subordinates had taken him: "I should like to know where they were when we were struggling against the colonialists. In those days I know the people went into combat as volunteers. These bandits kidnap people and force them to join them. I would rather they killed me than belong to them." (And he was kidnapped twice and twice managed to escape.)

I can see there are many questions I should put to this general, head of the assassins. But even if his head was spinning, I should not try to forget the question a little boy of eight put to his mother: "Mama, why do the bandits kill? Do the bandits have a country, Mama?"

Yes, I should not try to forget to put that question to that creature who leads murderers of defenseless children, old people, women, men and youngsters: Do they have a country? Do the bandits have a country?

Then later I should seek out those who deprive their people of the sweat of their labor—since it is the nameless people who produce wealth—that they then use to manufacture weapons or buy and deliver them to the murderous groups. I should ask what kind of war is this? Isn't it terrorism they carry out? Isn't it terrorism they promote by sheltering, arming and encouraging the armed bandits? Isn't it terrorism to assert that there is a civil war in Mozambique? And I should tell them the story told by one woman returning from captivity.

She was kidnapped on the outskirts of the city of Maputo, with her baby still suckling. Her child was crying, either hungry or upset by the long march which she and her mother were forced to endure.

The bandits felt threatened by the child's crying. They were afraid of being heard and reported to the armed forces. They were worried. They scolded the mother. They indicated that she should make the child shut up.

Among them, a bandit already, was a child who looked about ten (though perhaps a little older, as his growth was stunted by malnutrition). He proposed to his chiefs, "This child is making a lot of noise. Can I kill her?"

And the mother said that when she heard this she sweated with horror. She looked to see who was speaking and saw that it was a mere child. She thrust here breast into her baby's mouth. He sucked at the milk and fell asleep.

She ended, "I was lucky. What would have happened to the baby if she had not gone to sleep. How can a child be a killer? He spoke so coldly that I'd no doubt he'd have done it. . . . And they picked on me to be the chief's woman." She was weeping.

Notes

1. *New York Times*, July 22, 1987.
2. *Minneapolis Star and Tribune*, July 24, 1987.
3. *New York Times*, July 25, 1987.
4. UNICEF, *Children of the Front Line*, (New York, 1987).
5. *Ibid.*
6. United Nations, Office of the Special Coordinator for Emergency Relief Operations, "Press Brief," May, 1987.
7. Phyllis Johnson and David Martin, *Destructive Engagement* (Harare, 1986), pp 5-10. This interpretation was tacitly acknowledged by Evo Fernandes, until recently the MNR spokesperson in Europe. (Transcript of interview with Evo Fernandes, April 4, 1983.)
8. Gordon Winter, *Inside Boss* (Harmondsworth, 1981), p 545.
9. *Africa Confidential*, July 21, 1985; *Sunday Times*, January 26, 1975; *Domingo*, January 10, 1982.
10. Quoted in *Resistência Naçional de Moçambique* (MNR), "Comando Geral," Afonso Macacho Marceta Dhlakama, Supreme Commander, November 28, 1980.

11. Winter, *Inside Boss*, pp 545-547.
12. From the beginning of this century, the most salient feature of Portuguese colonialism was the absence of development capital. This lack provided South African investors with a strategic entry point from which to dominate the Mozambican economy. On the eve of independence, Mozambique's underdeveloped economy derived approximately half of all its hard currency from economic relations with South Africa.
13. Quoted in *Resistência Naçional de Moçambique* (MNR), "Comando Geral," Afonso Macacho Marceta Dhlakama, Supreme Commander, November 28, 1980.
14. SADCC stands for Southern African Coordination Conference. It was founded in 1980. For a detailed study of the SADCC, see Carol Thompson, *Challenge to Imperialism* (Harare, 1985), pp 258-294.
15. Colin Legum, "The Counter Revolutionaries in Southern Africa: The Challenge of the Mozambican Resistance," *Third World Reports* (March, 1983), p 2.
16. Quoted in *Ibid*, p 3.
17. For a discussion of Pretoria's shifting southern Africa strategy, see Robert Davies and Dan O'Meara, "Total Strategy in Southern Africa: An Analysis of South African Regional Policy Since 1978," *Journal of Southern Africa Studies*, II (1985): 185.
18. Quoted in *Resistência Naçional de Moçambique*, "Relatório Referente a Sessão do Trabalho de R.N.M. e do Representativo do Governo Sul Africano," October 25, 1980.
19. Phyllis Johnson and David Martin, *Destructive Engagement*, pp 36-37.
20. *Financial Times*, January 6, 1983; *Washington Post*, January 7, 1983; *Observer*, February 20, 1983.
21. On March 16, 1984, at the border town of Nkomati, Mozambique and South Africa signed an agreement in which each side formally promised "not to allow its territory to be used for acts of war, aggression or violence against the other state." From the outset, the apartheid regime violated the Nkomati accord by providing military assistance to the MNR. See Allen

110

Isaacman, "The Escalating Conflict in Southern Africa," *Survival* (forthcoming).

22. *Reuters*, August 22, 1982.
23. *Washington Post*, May 29, 1987.
24. Since the last third of the nineteenth century, migrant laborers from Mozambique have worked on the South African mines and plantations. On the eve of independence, approximately 100,000 were working in the gold mines and an equally large number was thought to have migrated clandestinely to the South African farms and in the cities. While the number of miners working in South Africa has dropped substantially, their presence as well as the presence of a large number of unregistered migratory workers provides a pool of potential recruits for the MNR. For a history of migratory labor to the South African mines, see Ruth First, *Black Gold* (Sussex, 1983).
25. Quoted in Allen Isaacman and Barbara Isaacman, "South Africa's Hidden War," *Africa Report* (November-December, 1982): 6.
26. Transcript of interview with John Burleson, May 27, 1982.
27. Quoted in *Africa News*, August 9, 1982.
28. Until now, there has been little evidence that the MNR has been able to build any meaningful social base in the countryside.

    The MNR has been trying to forge an alliance with some "traditional chiefs" who lost their official status and privileged colonial position at independence. To date, this strategy has yielded few tangible results and they are unlikely to do so. Although the institution of chieftancy or *regulo* was abolished only in 1975, well before then it had become devoid of any political meaning in most parts of the country. This came about as a result of the common colonial practice of replacing indigenous chiefs (who had spiritual responsibility both for the fertility of the land and the well-being of their subjects), with more pliant junior members of the royal family, African police (sepais), ex-colonial soldiers, and strangers (all of whom lacked historical legitimacy). In repayment for their services, the appointed chiefs and their heirs enjoyed a relatively privileged social and economic position, often predicated upon the exploitation of their subjects (see Allen Isaacman, "Chiefs, Rural Differentiations and Peasant Protest: The Mozambican Forced Cotton Regime, 1938–1961", *African Economic History* 14, [1985]: 15–56).

South Africa's surrogates have also made a concerted effort to "Africanize" their external leadership and to patch up deep and embarrassing rifts among those claiming to represent the MNR abroad.

29. U.S. Department of State, Current Policy No. 980, "Mozambique: Charting a New Course," July, 1987.
30. *Ibid.*
31. Immediately after the crash, a general consensus emerged suggesting that Machel's death was an accident. News accounts, coming primarily from South Africa, emphasized some combination of human error and bad weather. Shortly thereafter, South Africa's Foreign Minister, P.W. Botha, offered several alternative explanations which laid blame for the crash on drunken Soviet pilots and antiquated Russian navigational equipment. His speculation received substantial play in the Western press. Subsequent evidence called the initial reports into question and Botha admitted before an International Commission of Inquiry on January 26 that his initial charges were groundless.

Thus, several months after Machel's death, the exact cause remains unknown. While there is no firm evidence linking South Africa to the crash, Western journalists have raised a number of new questions which may never, given the fragmentary nature of the data and Pretoria's strict censorship policy, be answered. Why were South African security forces placed on full alert the night before Machel's crash? Why didn't South African controllers inform the Soviet pilot that he had entered South African territory? The controllers' silence is particularly puzzling since the South African journal, *Business Day* (October 21, 1986) has reported that they had tracked Machel's plane with a sophisticated computer-assisted radar system for hundreds of miles before it had entered the militarily sensitive region of the eastern Transvaal. And, finally, what was the origin of the radio beacon which, experts believed, drew the plane off course. Pretoria has suggested that it may have come from an airport in Swaziland, but it uses a different frequency from the Maputo airport which was the plane's destination. An alternative explanation published in the *New York Times* (January 27, 1987) suggests that the plane may have been drawn off course by decoy beams from South Africa. Reports from witnesses that a large tent, which could have housed mobile electronic equipment, stood 150 yards from where the plane went down and was dismantled the day after the crash, and the failure of the South African authorities to inform Mozambique of the crash for fifteen hours while they rifled through confidential documents have fueled speculation about the cause. So, too, have accounts of implicit threats against Machel made by South African Defense Chief Magnus Malan shortly before the crash and Machel's own revelation that there had already been an attempt on his life.

On July 9, 1987, the South African Board of Inquiry blamed the Soviet flight crew for the disaster and ignored or downplayed any evidence pointing to the South African military as the culprits. The Mozambican government rejected the conclusions and for the first time publicly declared its belief that Machel was murdered. *London Times*, July 10, 1987; *New York Times*, July 10, 1987; *Guardian*, July 29, 1987.

32. Interview with President Joaquim Chissano, June 5, 1987.